The most sublime mystery in the Christian faith is the incarnation of God in Christ. "The Word became flesh and blood, and moved into the neighborhood" (John 1:14), as Eugene Peterson's memorable translation puts it. Now Derek Vreeland has adapted *The Message* translation to lead us in a biblical exploration of the incarnation, crucifixion, and resurrection in a fresh way for small groups and individuals alike.

BRIAN ZAHND, author of *The Wood Between the Worlds*

Derek has accomplished something rare with the God in the Neighborhood Bible Studies. His work is rich and deep, saturated in Scripture and theologically sound, yet it also reveals a profound attention to the condition of our hearts. Through heartfelt prayers and spiritually attuned pastoral leadership, Derek invites us into the all-important work of Christlikeness. God in the Neighborhood is sure to deepen our affection for Christ and exhort us to enjoy closer fellowship with our incarnate, crucified, and risen Savior, Jesus.

KAT ARMSTRONG, Bible teacher, podcast host, and author of the **Storyline Bible Studies** series

Vreeland artfully guides us into Scripture's wild country, where we see with fresh eyes the wonder of the human God.

WINN COLLIER, pastor, director of the Eugene Peterson Center for Christian Imagination, and author of *A Burning in My Bones: The Authorized Biography of Eugene H. Peterson* and *Love Big, Be Well*

With theological depth and pastoral warmth, Derek Vreeland leads us into Scripture using the down-to-earth beauty of *The Message* translation to reveal the wonder of God made flesh. What I love most about this study is how it keeps our eyes on Jesus—God with us—and at the same time helps us imagine how that truth reshapes how we live with and for our neighbors. It is prophetic and hopeful, grounded and transformative.

JULIET LIU, pastor of Life on the Vine Christian Community

Derek Vreeland serves as a thoughtful guide in this excellent Bible study. I especially appreciate the way each lesson is structured in four sections, offering space for journaling and prayer. It's a rich resource—perfect for personal reflection as well as group study.

TIM WILDSMITH, pastor, professor, YouTuber, and author of *Bible Translations for Everyone* and *Daily Scripture Guidebook*

In the God in the Neighborhood Bible Studies, my friend Derek Vreeland opens up the heart of the gospel not as a collection of abstract doctrines but as the truth of God to be lived every moment, every day, wherever we are. *Incarnation* reveals God drawing near. *Crucifixion* displays God's self-giving love. *Resurrection* announces that hope is stronger than despair. These studies are grounded in the story of Scripture, pastoral in tone, and deeply practical. Derek writes as both a pastor and a friend, guiding us gently toward Jesus. As you work through these studies, you will find that God is not only in heaven above us but also alive in the laughter, sorrows, and stories of the place you call home.

TOMMY BROWN, author of *The Speed of Soul*

As Christians we know that Jesus is the face of God (2 Corinthians 4:6), which means that every contour of the Scripture is but the outline of the face of the incarnate, crucified, and resurrected one; the one in whom is all the fullness of the Godhead (Colossians 2:9), in whose presence we melt in adoration and worship. We believe this—but sometimes it is difficult to see. We need wise guides to help us not only recognize his face but also hear his voice and follow him where he goes—into the country of sin and death to seek and save the lost. I commend to you this series by Derek Vreeland—biblical, accessible, pastoral, wise. A resource that will edify believers old and new.

ANDREW ARNDT, lead pastor at New Life East and author of *A Strange and Gracious Light*

Anybody familiar with *The Message* translation has likely been moved by the idea of the Word that "became flesh and blood, and moved into the neighborhood" (John 1:14). It's one of those verses that begs for more reflection. With the God in the Neighborhood Bible Studies, Derek Vreeland has delivered on that impulse by leading us through reflections on the incarnation, crucifixion, and resurrection of Jesus Christ. These studies are not a survey in abstract theology; they are an invitation to consider what it means to be "in Christ"—the Christ who poured himself into the incarnation, who gave his life in redemptive work, and who rose in triumph over the order of death and darkness. This study will invigorate your partnership with the God who is still at work in our neighborhoods.

MARTY SOLOMON, author of *Asking Better Questions of the Bible* and creator of *The BEMA Podcast*

RESURRECTION

GOD IN THE NEIGHBORHOOD BIBLE STUDIES

8 Lessons on How God Restores Us

DEREK VREELAND

NavPress®

Published in alliance with Tyndale House Publishers

NavPress.com

Resurrection: 8 Lessons on How God Restores Us

A NavPress resource published in alliance with Tyndale House Publishers

The Team:
David Zimmerman, Publisher; Olivia Eldredge, Acquisitions Editor; Elizabeth Schroll, Copyeditor; Lacie Phillips, Production Assistant; Eva M. Winters, Designer; Sarah Ocenasek, Proofreading Coordinator

For information about special discounts for bulk purchases, please contact Tyndale House Publishers at csresponse@tyndale.com, or call 1-855-277-9400.

ISBN 978-1-64158-992-5

Printed in the United States of America

32 31 30 29 28 27 26
7 6 5 4 3 2 1

To Dylan

May you always do for others and let others do for you

CONTENTS

The Word became flesh and blood,
    and moved into the neighborhood.
We saw the glory with our own eyes,
    the one-of-a-kind glory,
    like Father, like Son,
Generous inside and out,
    true from start to finish.

JOHN 1:14

AS WE BEGIN

An Introduction to Resurrection

I recently sat at our local DMV, waiting on new license plates, and the guy sitting next to me started up a conversation. (Sadly, I'd left my AirPods at home. They would have given me a buffer to prevent a conversation I didn't want to have.) I acknowledged him initially with a comment about getting older and my two little grandchildren, but then I just got quiet while he talked about how everything feels like it's falling apart—the economy, crooked politicians, and whatever the people in charge had said on the news the night before. I stared at the ground and sighed deeply within myself but said nothing. Any affirmation would only plunge this conversation deeper into the darkness. Any comments to the contrary would only start an argument. I chose the third way—silence—because I knew that to dwell on the darkness with empty complaints would only give the devil a foothold in my heart.

I know it can feel like life is unstable and the darkness of corruption is spreading. It's not *completely* dark yet, but it seems like it's getting there. Admittedly, we see the darkness of moral corruption and injustice all around us—in our news feeds, in conversations with friends, and even in conversations with strangers at the DMV. The problems in our neighborhoods, compounded by the problems in the country we call home, are very real. But I won't let the darkness win. I won't let despair and hopelessness get the best of me. Our collective troubles tell a story of setbacks and loss, a story of pain and wrongdoing, but they do not tell the whole story.

The good news is that the Word came to live among us, determined to renew our neighborhoods. As the living Word of God, Jesus joins us in life, and we awaken to God's presence. He joins us in death, dying with us and for us, and we believe.

But he didn't remain in the tomb—the shackles of death couldn't bind him. On the third day, he rose again! Jesus joined us in new life, and we participate in what God is doing through Jesus to make all things new. The light of resurrection pushes back the darkness of despair.

The joy I feel throughout the season of Easter is not just because of Easter eggs, the Easter Bunny, and Easter Sunday services with a church full of worshipers. Every year, Easter reminds us that God has not abandoned God's good creation—the wide-open meadows; deep, dark forests; white-sand beaches; breathtaking mountain vistas; and especially human beings living together in neighborhoods. The resurrection of Jesus is the first sign that God's new-creation project is up and running. The current state of the world may be dark and growing darker, but the light of resurrection continues to shine through new beginnings and new life, like a flower growing through a sidewalk crack. So I refuse to allow despair's dark thoughts to dominate my imagination. I'm too busy participating in God's new creation.

When I look inside my own heart, I see this new life being produced. As Paul writes, "We look inside, and what we see is that anyone united with the Messiah gets a fresh start, is created new. The old life is gone; a new life emerges! Look at it!" (2 Corinthians 5:17). I recognize this paradigm created by Jesus' crucifixion and resurrection in my own life. The Christian life is a process of the old dying and the new being born. We grow into the likeness of King Jesus as our stubborn and rebellious old selves are crucified and our redeemed and restored new selves come to life. I can say with Paul, "I have been crucified with Christ" (Galatians 2:20). And just as I have been crucified, I have also been raised to new life with Christ.

The following eight lessons will prepare you to live this life of faith in the sure hope of the resurrection. We begin in the book of Job, where Job expresses his confidence—amid his suffering—in the God who can redeem and restore life. Lesson 2 takes us into the Gospels, where Jesus declares to Martha his identity as the embodiment of resurrection and life. Lesson 3 moves us into Paul's letter to the Romans, where he shows us how the resurrection of Jesus brings an end to the fear of death *as the end*.

Lesson 4 invites us as resurrection people to offer up to God our everyday, ordinary lives. Lesson 5 walks us through Paul's lengthy but important description of resurrection in 1 Corinthians 15, where he reveals how Jesus' victory over death is the linchpin of our faith. Lesson 6 challenges us to know Jesus in the power of his resurrection, not just know things *about* Jesus. Lesson 7 shows us how to live what Paul calls "this new resurrection life" (Colossians 3:1). Lesson 8 takes us to the end of the Bible, the book of Revelation, to see one final image of God making all things new.

This Bible study series uses the beauty and sacredness of ordinary language found in *The Message*, a contemporary and imaginative translation of the Bible, to lead you on a journey through the Scriptures to encounter Jesus in his life, death, and resurrection. The series is broken into three parts:

Book 1, *Incarnation*, dives deep into the mystery of the incarnation, where God meets us, joining us in life.

Book 2, *Crucifixion*, reflects on Jesus' execution, where God joins us in death, and in doing so, saves us.

Book 3, *Resurrection*, leads us on an Easter journey, where God joins us in life anew to restore us to what we were created to be: image bearers of the God of love.

When we realize that God is with us in life, we *come alive*. When we understand that God is with us in death, we *believe*. When we experience God-With-Us in new life, we *participate*. These studies are designed to bring you into "God's neighboring presence," a phrase I picked up from Eugene Peterson.[1] The coming of Jesus marks God moving into our neighborhood, and he is present with us as personally as any of our neighbors.

How to Use This Bible Study

Lessons in these Bible studies are designed for either individual reflection or group study in small groups, Sunday school classes, or home groups. You are invited to use these Bible studies for your own personal growth and spiritual formation. Lessons are made up of four parts—"The Approach," "The Word," "The Neighborhood," and "The Prayer." Here is how each lesson is structured.

The Approach: Setting the Scene

We begin with an introduction to the Scripture passage from *The Message* we will cover in each lesson. "The Approach" ends with starter questions to get you thinking (if you are reading on your own) or to help your group begin sharing with one another.

The Word: Diving into Scripture

Following our introduction and opening questions, we turn our attention to a particular passage of Scripture and dig in, looking at the uniqueness of the language of *The Message*. In his translation, Eugene Peterson sought to break down the dividing wall between so-called secular and so-called sacred language. For Peterson, *all* language is sacred because it is all a gift from God.[2] Questions are provided here, as well, to encourage you to enter the text more fully.

The Neighborhood: Living It Out

We will wrap up each lesson by looking outward toward our own neighborhoods, asking how the passage of Scripture calls us to live in the way of Jesus while we are among our real flesh-and-blood neighbors. Following Jesus is not merely gaining knowledge and categorizing God facts. Following Jesus is a way of living shaped by the Holy Spirit around the death and resurrection of Jesus so that our lives look like dying to self and rising to reflect the life of Jesus. Reflection questions guide this outward focus on how we live in our neighborhoods filled with real people who may or may not identify as Christians.

The Prayer: Drawing Near to God

Each lesson concludes with a prayer drawn from the specific Bible passage used in that lesson.

There are companion videos available on my website here:

Before You Start

If you are using these Bible studies on your own, find a quiet and comfortable place to read. Before you start a lesson, take a deep breath, exhale slowly, and offer a brief prayer. Ask the Holy Spirit to work with Holy Scripture to show you the ways of Jesus. As you are reading, feel free to jot down responses to the questions throughout each lesson.

If you are using these Bible studies in a group, take turns introducing yourself to the group; perhaps you could each share why you are in this Bible study or what you hope to get out of it. Open with prayer, asking Jesus to pour out the Holy Spirit on your group so that the Holy Spirit will be your teacher and guide. Identify a group leader to guide the conversation. Give people a few moments to reflect on the questions through the study, and then invite them to share with the group their thoughts and answers to the questions. Don't rush people to answer. Trust and learn from silence.

Whether you're doing this study on your own or in community, if you are able, read all Scripture passages out loud and pray the prayer at the end of each lesson aloud.

I love Jesus. I've loved Jesus since I was fifteen years old, and after all these years, I *still* love Jesus, because he never ceases to amaze and surprise me. And I love leading Bible studies, because when we take time to study Holy Scripture, God always surprises me with new details that make me ponder. My prayer is that you will grow in gratitude through these Bible studies and see with greater clarity what God has done for us in and through Jesus. I pray you will grow in your knowledge of the ways of Jesus and feel the nudging of the Holy Spirit to live out what you believe.

Derek Vreeland
Easter 2025

LESSON 1

THE ONE WHO GIVES ME BACK MY LIFE

The Approach

I believe, with deep conviction, in the literal and historical resurrection of Jesus.

Christians can discuss and debate what we believe about the proper mode of baptism, the gifts of the Holy Spirit, or the proper sequence of events regarding the end of this present age and not ever reach a place of perfect agreement, but Jesus' physical resurrection is an undeniable reality for Christian faith. It is the linchpin of our faith. Everything we believe rests on the account of Mary Magdalene and the apostles, who saw the risen Jesus with their own eyes. His resurrection changes everything, including how we look at the cross.

Without his resurrection, the crucifixion of Jesus looks like failure and defeat—a crucified king is a cursed king. In Galatians, Paul reminds us of the Scripture that says, "Cursed is everyone who hangs on a tree" (Galatians 3:13; Deuteronomy 21:22-23). However, the Spirit has vindicated Jesus and revealed his death as victorious.

While the ruling powers wanted to humiliate Jesus through crucifixion and stamp out his rival-Kingdom movement, God turned the cross into a throne, the place of Jesus' saving enthronement. Jesus' death defeats sin, death itself, and the power of the evil one. Through his resurrection, Jesus brings about new life—resurrection life—which marks the dawn of God's new creation. Jesus came bursting through the doors of death "leading the resurrection parade" (Colossians 1:18) and inviting us into restoration, where God is making all things new.

Jesus not only went down *into* death and came back to life; Jesus went all the way *through* death and came out on the other side, creating a gateway into a world of new creation.

By the first century, most, but not all, Jewish people believed that a resurrection would take place at the end of the age. Jews, Christians, and pagans of the first century understood the Greek word *anastasis* to mean something like new physical life after a time of real physical death. According to New Testament scholar N. T. Wright, "All of them were speaking of a new life *after* 'life after death' in the popular sense, a fresh living embodiment *following* a period of death-as-a-state." The word *resurrection* as used by followers of Jesus didn't mean metaphorical life after death but physical life on the earth, what Wright describes as "life *after* 'life after death.'"[1]

Jesus had told his disciples that he would be killed and on the third day he would rise, but none of them had the imagination to expect what happened on that first Easter Sunday. To understand how Jesus and the apostles viewed resurrection, we start in the Old Testament.

We don't find many detailed descriptions of resurrection in the Old Testament, like we see in Paul's letters, but we do find whispers of resurrection in some places. Here are a few of those hints:

> "'Many who have been long dead and buried will wake up, some to eternal life, others to eternal shame.
>
> "'Men and women who have lived wisely and well will shine brilliantly, like the cloudless, star-strewn night skies. And those who put others on the right path to life will glow like stars forever.'"
>
> DANIEL 12:2-3

But friends, your dead will live,
    your corpses will get to their feet.
All you dead and buried,
    wake up! Sing!
Your dew is morning dew
    catching the first rays of sun,
The earth bursting with life,
    giving birth to the dead.

ISAIAH 26:19

"Therefore, prophesy. Tell them, 'God, the Master, says: I'll dig up your graves and bring you out alive—O my people! Then I'll take you straight to the land of Israel. When I dig up graves and bring you out as my people, you'll realize that I am God. I'll breathe my life into you and you'll live. Then I'll lead you straight back to your land and you'll realize that I am God. I've said it and I'll do it. God's Decree.'"

EZEKIEL 37:12-14

It was upon this Old Testament foundation that Jesus came to join us in new life through his resurrection. Most Christians worship corporately on Sunday, the first day of the week, because Jesus rose from the dead on Sunday. In that sense, every Sunday is a celebration of the resurrection, but the season of Easter focuses our attention on the celebration of Jesus' resurrection for seven weeks. During Lent we fast, but during Easter we feast. Christ is risen and death has been conquered! We celebrate because the Kingdom has come and God's new-creation project is off and running!

Before we move on to look at an important resurrection passage in the Old Testament, reflect on the following questions.

1. What kind of Easter traditions did you celebrate when you were a child?

2. What are your thoughts about the Easter Bunny? Are you pro-Bunny? Anti-Bunny? Indifferent?

3. What is your go-to Easter candy?

The Word

Job falls within the Wisdom Literature section of the Old Testament, right before Psalms. The world created by the wise sayings of King Solomon in Proverbs operates under these steady principles: *Do good, live well, and you will experience good things.* Proverbs also warns us that, by contrast, if we choose the way of foolishness, evil, and laziness, life will not turn out so well. For example, "The wisdom of the wise keeps life on track; / the foolishness of fools lands them in the ditch" (Proverbs 14:8).

I appreciate the story of Job because it's a Spirit-inspired counterbalance to the voice we hear in Proverbs. While the wisdom of Proverbs is true in a general sense, Job comes along and says, "Hold on a second!"

Job *lived well* and *did good* but landed in a ditch of despair and suffering. Job "was honest inside and out, a man of his word, who was totally devoted to God and hated evil with a passion" (Job 1:1). He lived according to the exhortations of Proverbs, but he did not experience the fruitful results Proverbs promises.

Job lost his home, his health, and his heritage—that is, his children. His only remaining family member mentioned in the Scriptures is Job's angry and grieving wife, who questioned him, saying, "Still holding on to your precious integrity, are you? Curse God and be done with it!" (Job 2:9). Job's friends showed up, trying to convince him that he must have done something wrong. They were supposed to be his faithful friends, and instead they became his adversarial accusers.

Three of Job's so-called friends—Eliphaz, Bildad, and Zophar—came to visit. They each questioned Job's integrity in their own way, and at every turn, Job defended his innocence. Job called them "miserable comforters" and asked, "Is there no end to your windbag speeches? / What's your problem that you go on and on like this?" (Job 16:2-3). When Bildad made his case that those who revel in wickedness are punished with calamity (Job 18:5-21), Job responded with the hope he had, a hope that forecasted the promised resurrection, a promise we still cling to as followers of Jesus (Job 19:25-27).

> "My relatives and friends have all left;
> houseguests forget I ever existed.
> The servant girls treat me like a deadbeat off the street,
> look at me like they've never seen me before."
>
> JOB 19:14-15

Not only did Job lose his children, but he also felt the absence of family and *real* friends. Eliphaz, Bildad, and Zophar brought him no comfort. Former guests in Job's home ignored him. Even those who had served in Job's household treated him with contempt.

> "I call my attendant and he ignores me,
> ignores me even though I plead with him.
> My wife can't stand to be around me anymore.
> I'm repulsive to my family."
>
> JOB 19:16-17

Job even reached out to his attendant, the house servant who would have been closest to him, but heard nothing back. Job's wife survived the calamity that took their children, but she, too, brought Job no relief. She couldn't stand to even be in his presence. In another translation, Job laments, "My breath is repulsive to my wife" (Job 19:17, NLT).

> "Even street urchins despise me;
> when I come out, they taunt and jeer.
> Everyone I've ever been close to abhors me;
> my dearest loved ones reject me."
>
> JOB 19:18-19

The term *street urchins* refers to homeless children and youth who survive by picking pockets and committing other acts of thievery. Such children are seen in Charles Dickens's novel *Oliver Twist*. In nineteenth-century British culture, these troublesome homeless children were despised by many people. Yet when they appear in the book of Job, even they despise Job when he is out on the streets. Everyone had turned their backs on Job!

> "I'm nothing but a bag of bones;
> my life hangs by a thread.
>
> "Oh, friends, dear friends, take pity on me.
> God has come down hard on me!
> Do you have to be hard on me, too?
> Don't you ever tire of abusing me?"
>
> JOB 19:20 22

Despair had become Job's only friend. He felt like a "bag of bones," discarded with the morning's trash. Job's situation made him feel like God was against him. He certainly felt the contempt and accusations of his so-called friends. He felt that they, too, were against him. Not only had life been hard on him, but his friends, who he'd hoped would offer some relief, only showed up with abuse.

> "If only my words were written in a book—
> better yet, chiseled in stone!"
>
> JOB 19:23-24

Job speaks with the heartbreaking voice of suffering, foreshadowing Jesus' anguished words on Good Friday as he cried out, "My God, my God, why have you abandoned me?" (Matthew 27:46). Job wanted his words of anguish recorded because he felt like his life was coming to an end.

> "Still, I know that God lives—the One who gives me back my life—
> and eventually he'll take his stand on earth.
> And I'll see him—even though I get skinned alive!—
> see God myself, with my very own eyes.
> Oh, how I long for that day!"
>
> JOB 19:25-27

In his reply to Bildad, Job unknowingly moves us from Good Friday to Easter Sunday—from despair to hope. He doesn't share our vantage point as readers of this story; what Job could not see was that it was not God who had taken away his family or inflicted terrible sores upon his skin. The hand that was hard against Job was that of Satan, the accuser, the enemy of God. Job assumed God had taken away his life but would one day give it back, when the truth of the matter is that Satan had taken away Job's life but God had plans to restore it. We can take hope that what the devil has stolen God will return in the end.

Somehow, despite all he endured, Job believed he would see God with his own eyes. He trusted in God as the one who would give him back his life. He felt his own impending death but believed in a new, real, bodily life *after* life after death. The New Living Translation brings out the physical nature of Job's hope: "After my body has decayed, / yet in my body I will see God!" (Job 19:26, NLT). In Jesus and through Jesus' resurrection, Job's hope would come to fruition.

With these words in mind, take a moment to reflect on the following questions.

4. What are the key differences between the world envisioned by the wisdom of Proverbs and the world seen through the suffering of Job?

5. Why do we have the tendency to blame God when things are not going our way?

6. As followers of Jesus, what are we to do in moments of suffering?

7. How does the promise of future embodied resurrection give suffering people hope today?

8. As you reflect on what God has done for you in the past, what are you most grateful for?

The Neighborhood

Sitting with the renewed hope that God will give us back our lives awakens in us a new dream for our neighborhoods. Who are the people society might write off as "street urchins"? Who are the people in your neighborhood who are overlooked or marginalized? Perhaps these people cause problems or create disturbances, or perhaps they are just ignored. Maybe they are children, teenagers, middle-aged divorcées, or lonely retirees. Can you see Jesus in them? Jesus taught us that whenever we show compassion to "someone overlooked or ignored, that was me—you did it to me" (Matthew 25:40). The people God puts in our neighborhoods are not just those we have friendly relationships with but also those who are overlooked and ignored.

9. How can you identify those without privilege who society has cast aside or who are marginalized from majority culture?

10. What can you do to help them yourself or connect them to local churches or organizations who can help them?

The Prayer

With your thoughts on your neighborhood, offer this prayer.

God of all compassion and grace, we thank you for joining us in new life. We thank you for the resurrection of Jesus, which undoes death and opens a door into a world you are making new. We pray for those in our neighborhoods who are overlooked. Help us see you in them. Help us extend the same grace you are extending to them. In the name of Jesus we humbly pray, amen.

LESSON 2

I AM, RIGHT NOW, RESURRECTION AND LIFE

The Approach

I used to have a strong aversion to funerals.

I only remember attending one funeral service as a child, for a family friend. That experience was disorienting. I recall my apprehension when standing in line to view our deceased friend, who was lying in an open casket. I didn't want to be there. I didn't want to view the body. I took a quick glance and quickly averted my eyes. During the funeral service, my mind wandered, taking me to any other place but there. I sat stoically, keeping a firm grip on my emotions, which I had completely shut down (an unhealthy habit that would take me years to unlearn).

As a young adult, I had no desire to view the body of my grandfather after he passed away. I was on the way to the airport when I received the call that he had died, my cell phone ringing as I exited the interstate. I was headed to Colorado to help lead a retreat, and my dad and I discussed funeral plans. I quickly dismissed the formality of joining in on the family viewing. I wrestled with whether to cut my trip short to attend the funeral service. In the end, I returned home early to be at the funeral. In those days, I avoided funerals when I had the power to choose, but I recognized the value of being present for my extended family. Gatherings prompted by the deaths of people we love—whether they be memorial services, funerals, or the popular "celebration of life" alternative—provide our communities space to grieve in moments of loss.

Describing the final days of her husband's life, Canadian author Karen Stiller writes, "In the valley of the shadow of death, I feared evil. I tried to believe that the Shepherd was with us because to not believe would be worse. I knew that. But the rod and the staff, they did not comfort me. . . . But I came to understand early on that God's comfort can arrive most obviously, for me at least, in the shape of other people." Stiller continues, "The church, family, friends, neighbors, the guy who shovels our driveway—they all emerged from the valley sides carrying tiny bits of light. The Shepherd was present, I thought I saw, in the noble bakers, the knitters of prayer shawls, the people who cleaned our house, the lasagna and chili makers. In the valley of the shadow of death, there is so much lasagna."[1] As followers of Jesus, we are called to surround those who are grieving with hope, made known through small acts of love and kindness.

As a pastor, my role is not so much to cook the lasagna but to be present, to pray, and (often) to officiate funeral services. These days I'm glad to attend funerals, even when I am not leading the service; I've learned that when life becomes disorienting for those who have experienced loss the best we can do as the church is simply show up and be present.

When I'm not officiating a funeral service, I have a habit of counting references to heaven and to resurrection.

Most of the time *heaven* easily outnumbers *resurrection* ten to one.

We certainly do have the hope of heaven. To be absent from our physical bodies is to be present with the Lord. "Yes, we are fully confident," writes the apostle Paul, "and we would rather be away from these earthly bodies, for then we will be at home with the Lord" (2 Corinthians 5:8, NLT). The Lord dwells in heaven, and we have a home there, but it is a *temporary* home. Our true and lasting home will be on the earth with the God of heaven when everything's made new and we rise in newly resurrected bodies. The hope that has encouraged Christians for two thousand years is not so much that we are going to heaven but that heaven is coming to earth. Jesus is moving into the neighborhood for the final time, and in that moment we will be changed. Our perishable bodies, subjected to death, will put on the imperishable; the mortal will put on immortality (1 Corinthians 15:53)! We will receive new, glorified bodies, and those who have died in faith will rise to new embodied life.

Take a moment to reflect on the following questions.

1. Do you remember the first funeral you attended? What details do you recall?

2. What has your personal experience with grief been like? Has the presence of others brought you comfort, or have you needed to process things alone?

3. What are the differences between the hope of heaven and the hope of resurrection?

The Word

During his earthly ministry, Jesus had a loyal group of disciples, followers, and admirers. He had his fair share of critics, but he also had friends. Among them were Mary, Martha, and their brother, Lazarus. They lived in Bethany, a village just down the road from Jerusalem. Jesus found himself in their home from time to time, most notably the time described in Luke 10, when Martha busied herself with all she had to do in the kitchen while Mary sat at Jesus' feet "hanging on every word he said" (Luke 10:39). Martha insisted that Jesus tell Mary to help her in the kitchen, but Jesus commended Mary for choosing to do the one essential thing.

At some point later, Lazarus became very ill, and Mary and Martha quickly got word to Jesus and his disciples, who were ministering near the Jordan River, miles away. From here we pick up the story in John 11.

> When Jesus got the message, he said, "This sickness is not fatal. It will become an occasion to show God's glory by glorifying God's Son."
>
> Jesus loved Martha and her sister and Lazarus, but oddly, when he heard that Lazarus was sick, he stayed on where he was for two more days.
>
> JOHN 11:4-6

Jesus' disciples didn't know how Jesus knew that death would not be the end of Lazarus's story at this time. What they did know was that he loved this family, both Lazarus, who was sick, and his sisters, who had notified Jesus. His love for this family—which John makes clear was undying and unconditional—was an intimate kind of friendship love, so it's surprising that Jesus waited two more days before going to Bethany.

> After the two days, he said to his disciples, "Let's go back to Judea."
>
> They said, "Rabbi, you can't do that. The Jews are out to kill you, and you're going back?"
>
> Jesus replied, "Are there not twelve hours of daylight? Anyone who walks in daylight doesn't stumble because there's plenty of light from the sun. Walking at night, he might very well stumble because he can't see where he's going."
>
> JOHN 11:7-10

We learn earlier in John that the Judean leaders, scribes, and Pharisees living in Judea had been plotting to kill Jesus for some time: "Jesus was going about his business in Galilee. He didn't want to travel in Judea because the Jews there were looking for a chance to kill him. It was near the time of Tabernacles, a feast observed annually by the Jews" (John 7:1-2). The Judean leaders living in and around Jerusalem wanted to take Jesus out. His disciples knew it and feared for him.

> He said these things, and then announced, "Our friend Lazarus has fallen asleep. I'm going to wake him up."
>
> The disciples said, "Master, if he's gone to sleep, he'll get a good rest and wake up feeling fine." Jesus was talking about death, while his disciples thought he was talking about taking a nap.
>
> Then Jesus became explicit: "Lazarus died. And I am glad for your sakes that I wasn't there. You're about to be given new grounds for believing. Now let's go to him."
>
> JOHN 11:11-15

Sleep had become a helpful metaphor for death in the first-century Jewish world because death in this age was known to be temporary. For example, Isaiah had written, "Those who die in the LORD will live; / their bodies will rise again! / Those who sleep in the earth / will rise up and sing for joy!" (Isaiah 26:19, NLT). Belief in a bodily resurrection at the end of the age had grown steadily, so by the time of Jesus' earthly ministry, most Jewish people looked forward to this rising up! The hope of early believers, rooted in the goodness of the one Creator-God, was that in death they would all sleep until they were raised to new life.

> That's when Thomas, the one called the Twin, said to his companions, "Come along. We might as well die with him."
>
> When Jesus finally got there, he found Lazarus already four days dead. Bethany was near Jerusalem, only a couple of miles away, and many of the Jews were visiting Martha and Mary, sympathizing with them over their brother. Martha heard Jesus was coming and went out to meet him. Mary remained in the house.
>
> JOHN 11:16-20

Lazarus had indeed died. When Jesus and his disciples arrived, Mary, who had previously sat at the Lord's feet, stayed in the house, perhaps to continue to grieve. Martha, on the other hand, hurriedly left the house to meet Jesus on the road, where the two of them had an important and impassioned conversation.

> Martha said, "Master, if you'd been here, my brother wouldn't have died. Even now, I know that whatever you ask God he will give you."
>
> Jesus said, "Your brother will be raised up."
>
> Martha replied, "I know that he will be raised up in the resurrection at the end of time."
>
> JOHN 11:21-24

Martha spoke honestly from a place of grief. Her sorrow was real. But Jesus spoke from a place of hope. In the end, his hope would triumph and heal her of her grief.

> "You don't have to wait for the End. I am, right now, Resurrection and Life. The one who believes in me, even though he or she dies, will live. And everyone who lives believing in me does not ultimately die at all. Do you believe this?"
>
> JOHN 11:25-26

The future had broken into the present. The resurrection coming at the end of time was now standing right in front of Martha. Not only would Jesus be "raised from the dead by the power of the Holy Spirit" (Romans 1:4, NLT) in the future; Jesus stood before Martha as the power of life and resurrection in human flesh then. Jesus invites us to new life through his resurrection, and Jesus embodied this new life in his incarnation. The hope of new life on the other side of death proclaimed by Jesus invited Martha into the tension between grief and trust. Would she have the capacity to believe this?

> "Yes, Master. All along I have believed that you are the Messiah, the Son of God who comes into the world."
>
> JOHN 11:27

Martha believed. Like many women in the New Testament, she believed in Jesus and has been presented to us as a model of faith. Mary, Martha's sister, believed too. She had chosen the one essential thing by sitting at Jesus' feet (Luke 10:38-42). Martha's confession of faith opened the door for her to receive God's work of salvation—Jesus proclaiming the ultimate defeat of death itself.

Take a moment to reflect on the following questions.

4. Who have been your friends as you have grown in the Christian faith?

5. When was the last time you had an important and impassioned conversation with Jesus? What do you need to talk to him about right now?

6. In what ways is death like sleep?

7. How does Jesus' declaration that he is Resurrection and Life give you hope when you consider the shortness of life?

8. Why do followers of Jesus sometimes wrestle with believing Jesus when they walk through the valley of the shadow of death? How have you struggled with hope in the face of death?

The Neighborhood

We live in cities of lonesome fear. While death will come to all our neighborhoods, the fear of death need not paralyze us. When we, like Martha, believe Jesus is, right now, Resurrection and Life, then we become hopeful resurrection people. Through faith in Jesus, we are formed into life-giving people who can enter the grief of our neighborhoods with the hope of resurrection.

9. How does the hope of resurrection change how you pray for your neighbors?

10. What is one act of kindness you can offer the next time there is a death in your neighborhood?

The Prayer

In the spirit of Martha's faith, offer this brief prayer.

Lord Jesus, we believe you are, right now, Resurrection and Life. We believe you are the King who has come into the world to vanquish death and embody new life. We want to participate in what you are doing in our neighborhoods, to offer life in the face of death, love in the face of fear, and hope in the face of despair. Form us into life-giving resurrection people. We ask this for your name's sake. Amen.

LESSON 3

OUR NEW GRACE-SOVEREIGN COUNTRY

The Approach

I have found value in accepting my own fragile mortality.

Grief brings a surprising kind of sorrow when we refuse to face the fact that immortality is not an inherent human trait; it is a gift from God. At the end of our lives, we will take one final breath in this world before we step into the world to come. Accepting the inevitability of death doesn't eliminate the grief we experience when someone we know dies, but it does help us face our own mortality. We ride the wave of emotions associated with grief to pass through its intensity, which helps us find closure. The five stages of grief described by Elisabeth Kübler-Ross have been well documented though not universally accepted and applied.[1] In no particular order, the five stages of grief are denial, anger, bargaining, depression, and acceptance.

David Kessler, a student and protégé of Kübler-Ross, adds a sixth stage—meaning. By "meaning," Kessler is not suggesting a clear understanding of the reasons why a person has died. He does not imply that death offers some kind of intrinsic meaning within itself but rather that meaning is what we create in the process of grieving. Kessler suggests, "Your loss is not a test, a lesson, something to handle, a gift, or a blessing. Loss is simply what happens to you in life. Meaning is what *you* make happen."[2]

When we construct meaning from tragedy and loss, we find a way to incorporate the grief into our lives rather than being overtaken by it. Moreover, doing this helps us accept the shortness of our lives, acknowledging the truth found in James 4:14, that "you're nothing but a wisp of fog, catching a brief bit of sun before disappearing." Life is undeniably short, but the hope given to us in the resurrection is that death is not the end. Death is a time of separation—indeed, a tearful goodbye—but as followers of Jesus we find meaning *in* and *through* the resurrection of Jesus, who leads us into new life. Facing the brevity of our lives prompts us to reorder our priorities. When we refuse to do so, we are tempted to chase passing pleasures and temporary delights.

Some people go the route of *denial.* They close their eyes, stick their fingers in their ears, and refuse to consider even the slightest thought of death. They have absorbed the modern Western world's death-denying posture of refusing to look honestly at the frailty of human life. In the words of Walter Brueggemann, these people have been unknowingly "schooled in denial" regarding the reality of death and dying as a present part of the human condition.[3] We have a poor habit of covering up our fears and insecurities with empty clichés and statements of certitude that distract us from the truth. Denying death makes the shock of grief much more jolting.

Some people go the route of *debauchery.* They look to fulfill sensual desires, assuming that if we are all going to die then we should first live it up. The apostle Paul tips his hat toward this approach, admitting, "If there's no resurrection, 'We eat, we drink, the next day we die,' and that's all there is to it" (1 Corinthians 15:32). The way of debauchery is the dark side of the *carpe diem* approach to life. (*Carpe diem* is a Latin phrase meaning "seize the day," made popular in the 1989 film *Dead Poets Society*, featuring Robin Williams.) The road paved with debauchery always leads to the dead end of despair.

Some people go the route of *discipline.* This course of action goes in the opposite direction of debauchery. Those who go the way of discipline recognize their impending deaths and do what they can to live as long as they can. They dedicate themselves to the gym and whatever fad diets and supplements are on the market, searching for the elusive fountain of youth. I see the value in a disciplined life but not in discipline for its own sake or for the sake of denial. While eating well and exercising are noble and necessary for living the good life God has for us, the discipline approach can also be a way of hiding from the inevitable.

As for me, I want to go the way of *discipleship*. To be disciples of Jesus requires that we take up our crosses and die to our false selves that we might rise to new life and be our true selves. I want us to follow Jesus into his crucifixion and death so that we might die to sin and walk in the newness of life without the fear of death. Jesus leads us out of that old country, where death reigns supreme. The resurrection life of Jesus invites us to look at death soberly but not hopelessly. As we walk with Jesus in resurrection life, we find a new country, where grace reigns and God the Holy Spirit transforms us into people of confidence and hope.

Take a moment to reflect on the following questions.

1. Which of the four options—denial, debauchery, discipline, or discipleship—do you see most people taking when faced with their mortality? Is there another path to take?

2. In what ways have we been schooled in denial?

3. What thoughts or emotions surface when you consider your own mortality, acknowledging that one day you will take your last breath?

The Word

Reflecting on the shortness of life and the inevitability of death puts us in a position to see the glory of Jesus' resurrection and consider how we should live as followers of Jesus. In Romans 6:1, Paul asks, "So what do we do?" Before we work our way through Romans 6:1-11, let's back up and look at the context in Romans 5. Paul's opening question may be short, but it's important! It's a rhetorical question that follows Paul's beautiful description of the death of Jesus in the previous chapter. Paul writes, "God put his love on the line for us by offering his Son in sacrificial death while we were of no use whatever to him" (Romans 5:8). The cross is both rescuing and revealing. One of the things God reveals to us through the death of Jesus is what love looks like.

Through an act of love, Jesus rescues us from the state of disagreement with God, what Paul calls "being at odds with God" (Romans 5:9). The problem for which the cross is the solution isn't primarily that *God* is at odds with us and has boiling anger toward sinful people, an anger that must be dealt with. The problem solved by Jesus' death is that *we* are at odds with God because of our failure to properly love God and neighbor. As humanity's representative, the Word has "moved into the neighborhood" (John 1:14) to give us a new start. Adam "got us in all this trouble with sin and death" (Romans 5:18), but *Jesus* got us out of trouble, and *Jesus* led us into new life. With this in the background, let's look at Romans 6.

> So what do we do? Keep on sinning so God can keep on forgiving? I should hope not! If we've left the country where sin is sovereign, how can we still live in our old house there? Or didn't you realize we packed up and left there for good? That is what happened in baptism. When we went under the water, we left the old country of sin behind; when we came up out of the water, we entered into the new country of grace—a new life in a new land!
>
> ROMANS 6:1-3

Jesus' blood was "poured out for many people / for the forgiveness of sins" (Matthew 26:28). His death demonstrates the love of God and sets us right with God. So should we keep on sinning knowing God forgives? Paul's response, as translated in *The Message*, is "I should hope not!" (Romans 6:2). This phrase is an emotionally charged and negative response to remind us that Jesus' blood not only *forgives* us of our sins but also *frees* us from sin—to ignore this is to move back into bondage to sin. As free people we move from the land of slavery to sin into the country of unfettered grace.

> That's what baptism into the life of Jesus means. When we are lowered into the water, it is like the burial of Jesus; when we are raised up out of the water, it is like the resurrection of Jesus. Each of us is raised into a light-filled world by our Father so that we can see where we're going in our new grace-sovereign country.
>
> ROMANS 6:3-5

Through baptism, we discovery our true identity in Jesus' death and resurrection. The water of baptism connects us to the dying and rising again of Jesus. It marks the permanent move from the old country of sin to the new country of grace. In that move, we die to our old identities and our old ways of thinking about ourselves and others. We are raised with Jesus out of the darkness of death and into the light of God's new country, one ruled by grace. The light of God's grace allows us to distinguish between truth and falsehood, goodness and wickedness, beauty and evil. Now that we can see, we can no longer keep living as if we are in the dark.

> Could it be any clearer? Our old way of life was nailed to the cross with Christ, a decisive end to that sin-miserable life—no longer captive to sin's demands! What we believe is this: If we get included in Christ's sin-conquering death, we also get included in his life-saving resurrection.
>
> ROMANS 6:6-8

Through faith and baptism, we get to share in Jesus' sin-conquering death and life-saving resurrection. We can no longer shuffle along in our old lives, our "sin-miserable" lives, because we have been set free from that old existence. Moreover, we no longer need to live with the fear of death. Jesus' own death defeated the ominous, lurking specter of death once and for all. Jesus' resurrection restored life, and those of us who believe are included in that restoration.

> We know that when Jesus was raised from the dead it was a signal of the end of death-as-the-end. Never again will death have the last word.
>
> ROMANS 6:9

So much of the fear surrounding death is the sense of its cruel finality. Our God has given us an innate instinct to seek out life, to preserve and endure; death runs counter to that instinct. It seems so wrong. But the resurrection of Jesus marked "the end of death-as-the-end." Jesus will have the last word, not death! The wrongness of death has been made right by Jesus' resurrection.

> When Jesus died, he took sin down with him, but alive he brings God down to us. From now on, think of it this way: Sin speaks a dead language that means nothing to you; God speaks your mother tongue, and you hang on every word. You are dead to sin and alive to God. That's what Jesus did.
>
> ROMANS 6:10-11

In this move from a land dominated by sin to our grace-sovereign country, we learn a new language: the language of life. God speaks this language. God formed the universe and all living things with the word of life. In this new country, sin and death are dead. With these deaths in view, we are free to live as God intended.

Take a moment to reflect on the following questions.

4. Why might people want to go on sinning after coming to Jesus and tasting the goodness of God?

5. Have you been baptized? If so, what was your baptism experience like? If not, what steps would you need to take to pursue baptism?

6. If sin has been defeated, if we are indeed dead to sin, why do we continue to get caught up in it?

7. What thoughts or feelings arise when you reflect on Romans 6:9: "We know that when Jesus was raised from the dead it was a signal of the end of death-as-the-end. Never again will death have the last word"?

8. What is a proper Christian response to the fear of death?

The Neighborhood

What are we to do with the people we know who are still stuck in a world dominated by sin and the fear of death? It seems like too often Christians have made the mistake of taking on a posture of contempt, crossing their arms tightly, rolling their eyes, and dismissing those who have not learned to speak the language of life. Grace doesn't empower us to stand up to judge. Grace empowers us to stoop down to help. The Word moved into the neighborhood to save, to restore . . . to help! In the end Jesus will judge, but presently Jesus is at work in our neighborhoods to rescue those beat up and broken by sin. Our calling is to work with Jesus in this regard.

9. In what ways have you learned to speak the new language of life in this grace-sovereign country?

10. Who in your family, circle of friends, or neighborhood needs help refocusing their identity around the resurrection of Jesus?

The Prayer

Offer this brief prayer as you consider how to help your neighbors.

Lord Jesus, you have defeated death, once and for all, and in doing so you have delivered us out of a sin-dominated country. We pray for those we know who are still stuck in that old country. Lead us in the ways of rescue. Show us how to offer assistance. Strengthen our hands that they may be extended to help. Bless our lips that they may speak words of life. This we pray for your name's sake. Amen.

LESSON 4

YOUR EVERYDAY, ORDINARY LIFE

The Approach

I'm convinced we are surrounded by beauty even if, at first glance, we don't see it.

The challenge before us is to capture beauty when we find it and store it up in our hearts. I've worked hard over the years to develop an attitude and habits that help me find beauty in the things God has made, specifically things found in my neighborhood, like the first blooms of spring or freshly fallen snow during winter. My eyes are drawn to brilliant blue skies in summertime and the changing colors of leaves as summer gives way to fall. I love getting out early in the summer months for long runs, leaving my house in the dark to beat the summer heat and then meeting the sunrise when it comes.

I find beauty not only in God's good creation but also in little things throughout my day, like a well-prepared meal with family or friends, the turning of the crisp pages of a new book, or the joy of watching old, familiar movies. One constant source of beauty found in my everyday, ordinary life is well-made coffee. I repeatedly tell people that I am not a coffee snob (admittedly, that is exactly what a coffee snob would say!), but I do grind my own beans and use a French press to make my morning coffee.

Coffee preparation has become an essential daily liturgy for me. It begins when I fill my kettle with filtered water, which I then place on the stove. While waiting for the water to boil, I pour beans into my grinder. After grinding the beans, I open the grinder and pause for a moment to take in the aroma. I scoop the grounds into my glass French press and wait. Upon the kettle's whistle, I remove the kettle from the heat and slowly count to thirty, allowing the water to reach the proper temperature. I carefully pour the water into the French press with a deliberate swirl motion. Once the French press is full, I stir vigorously with a wooden spoon, close the lid, and wait.

I open the cabinet door to select my coffee cup; it can change from time to time, but normally I use my "First Presbyterian Church—Americus, Georgia" cup, a gift from a pastor friend nearly twenty years ago. Waiting for the coffee to steep is the longest four minutes of my day. When the coffee is ready, I push down the plunger on the French press, pour the fully brewed coffee into my cup, and watch little bubbles appear on the surface. Then, at long last, I take that first sip and enjoy the magic. The beauty of this ordinary moment rarely escapes me. While it is a simple process, I treasure my daily liturgy every morning—not just that day's cup but the thought of every new cup to follow.

We fill most of the hours of the day with ordinary tasks, ordinary conversations, and ordinary experiences. As followers of Jesus, we are to discover distinctly Christian ways to live an ordinary life. Our shared Christian experience isn't merely a matter of *believing new things* about God in the light of Jesus' death and resurrection. It's about *living a new way* in the light created by Jesus' resurrection. Jesus rose from the dead not only so we would *think* differently—he was raised that we might *live* differently. As we saw in our last lesson, we were raised to a new life with Jesus, so "now we also may live new lives" (Romans 6:4, NLT).

God the Holy Spirit works to transform us from the inside out, molding and conforming our internal desires to align with the commands to love God and neighbor, so that love becomes the way we live. While moral dilemmas stand at the door in both the everyday and the exceptional moments of life, the choice of love becomes an instinct for those of us who have been formed in love.

Take a moment to reflect on the following questions.

1. Are you more of a morning person or a night person? Are you more excited about catching a sunrise or a sunset?

2. What are some of the beautiful things about your everyday life?

3. What are the problems with *thinking* differently about God but not *living* differently because of Jesus' resurrection?

The Word

The book of Romans is by far Paul's most intricate and theologically robust letter. His winding and interwoven argument for the gospel as the unifying announcement for both Jewish and non-Jewish people can be divided up into four sections—chapters 1–4, chapters 5–8, chapters 9–11, and chapters 12–16.[1]

The opening four chapters reveal God's righteousness. Chapters 5–8 describe the nature of God's new covenant through Jesus and the coming of the Spirit. Chapters 9–11 deal with God's faithfulness despite Israel's unbelief. Upon this complex foundation, Paul begins his pastoral exhortations for the multiethnic church in chapter 12 with an emphatic "So here's what I want you to do" (Romans 12:1). While the previous eleven chapters form one dense, important theological argument, chapter 12 spells out how we should live based on Paul's case for the gospel.

> So here's what I want you to do, God helping you: Take your everyday, ordinary life—your sleeping, eating, going-to-work, and walking-around life—and place it before God as an offering. Embracing what God does for you is the best thing you can do for him.
>
> ROMANS 12:1

This is a very imaginative and unique translation of a very familiar verse. While other translations of Romans 12:1 read "present your bodies" (NRSV) or "give your bodies" (NLT), *The Message* describes the ordinary things we do with our bodies. In this translation, "bodies" are understood figuratively, as in what we do with our bodies—things like sleeping, eating, going to work, and walking around. This translation is consistent with Paul's intention in this passage. Paul doesn't mean that we are to literally sacrifice our physical bodies as offerings to God. The final line of this verse is often translated "which is your spiritual worship" (NRSV), while *The Message* offers a different insightful way of thinking about worship. What makes worship *spiritual*? It's embracing what God does for you. Spiritual worship begins when we stop striving to reach God and start receiving what God has done for us by grace.

The invitation to new life, through the death and resurrection of Jesus, is what God has done for us! We embrace new life by allowing our everyday, ordinary lives to be transformed by the death and resurrection of Jesus.

> Don't become so well-adjusted to your culture that you fit into it without even thinking. Instead, fix your attention on God. You'll be changed from the inside out. Readily recognize what he wants from you, and quickly respond to it. Unlike the culture around you, always dragging you down to its level of immaturity, God brings the best out of you, develops well-formed maturity in you.
>
> ROMANS 12:2

The temptation of the people of God from the beginning has been to become well-adjusted to the pagan culture around us. A worldly culture conforms us into its immaturity, but God the Holy Spirit transforms us into maturity—that is, "to the full and complete standard of Christ" (Ephesians 4:13, NLT). Part of the process of this maturity is letting go of simplistic religious clichés and accepting that the truth we find in Jesus is much more complex and nuanced than we first thought.

Moving down to verse 9, we encounter a list of things we can do to live in the light created by Jesus' resurrection. These core Christian practices are some of the ways we can give God our everyday, ordinary lives and resist the pressure to become like the culture around us.

> Love from the center of who you are; don't fake it. Run for dear life from evil; hold on for dear life to good. Be good friends who love deeply; practice playing second fiddle.
>
> Don't burn out; keep yourselves fueled and aflame. Be alert servants of the Master, cheerfully expectant. Don't quit in hard times; pray all the harder. Help needy Christians; be inventive in hospitality.
>
> ROMANS 12:9-13

To love authentically from the core of who we are is the essence of Christian spirituality. We don't become more like Jesus by faking it. Our connectivity to the presence of God keeps us honest and authentic, fueled and aflame with the love of God. Most of the practices of prayer have been given to us to help us remain alert and aware of the presence of God.

> Bless your enemies; no cursing under your breath.
>
> ROMANS 12:14

We don't curse our enemies. We love them because, as hard as it is to imagine sometimes, God loves them too. God loves the people we want to hate. Jesus taught us that when we love our enemies we are acting like our Father in heaven, who "is kind to those who are unthankful and wicked" (Luke 6:35, NLT).

> Laugh with your happy friends when they're happy; share tears when they're down. Get along with each other; don't be stuck-up. Make friends with nobodies; don't be the great somebody.
>
> ROMANS 12:15-16

We practice love in the life of the local church. We join in the joys and struggles of our brothers and sisters in Christ. When we discover something to celebrate, we laugh together, and when the walls surrounding our lives begin to close in on us, we weep together. The way of Jesus is not the way of self-aggrandizement. It's the way of humility.

> Don't hit back; discover beauty in everyone. If you've got it in you, get along with everybody. Don't insist on getting even; that's not for you to do. "I'll do the judging," says God. "I'll take care of it."
>
> ROMANS 12:17-19

We live as a nonretaliatory people because the peace of Jesus doesn't come through fighting or revenge but in cosuffering love and peacemaking. We practice forgiveness because we know that in the end God will take care of those who do wrong.

> Our Scriptures tell us that if you see your enemy hungry, go buy that person lunch, or if he's thirsty, get him a drink. Your generosity will surprise him with goodness. Don't let evil get the best of you; get the best of evil by doing good.
>
> ROMANS 12:20-21

When we try to fight evil with evil, we multiply evil. We remain in darkness, but Jesus has led us out into the light of God's love through his resurrection. He has rescued us from a culture of revenge and retaliation and brought us into God's grace-sovereign country! Getting the best of evil by doing good is one of the many ways we can bring our everyday, ordinary lives to God as offerings.

Take a moment to reflect on the following questions.

4. Consider the statement "Love from the center of who you are." What does that idea communicate to you about the nature of Christian love?

5. What do you do when you know you are called to love but you struggle to be loving in a certain situation?

6. What does it look like to "[play] second fiddle"? What does that image communicate?

7. What keeps us from burning out in this faith journey we are on?

8. What are some habits we can practice to become the kind of people who can love and bless our enemies?

The Neighborhood

How we respond to our unpleasant neighbors, the inconsiderate and rude ones, says more about our level of Christian maturity than how we worship on Sunday mornings does. God has placed us in neighborhoods to be salt and light, making people thirsty for the things of God and illuminating the presence of the Kingdom of God. We carry out this mission in what we do with ordinary interactions with those in our neighborhoods. We fulfill the ministry of Jesus not so much by preaching at them but by inviting them into our lives through practices of hospitality. We love all our neighbors and bless those who want to position themselves as enemies.

9. What are some inventive ways you can practice hospitality in your neighborhood?

10. What is the best way you can respond to enemies in your neighborhood?

The Prayer

Pause and reflect on the ordinary things in your day-to-day life. Take a deep breath. Exhale. Offer this brief prayer.

Creator-God, Giver of all good things and Maker of all beautiful things, we offer you the ordinary parts of our lives. We give them to you as an act of worship. Breathe the breath of life into our ordinary days. Empower us to be outposts of the Kingdom of God in our neighborhoods, known for our love, hospitality, compassion, and empathy. In Jesus' name we pray, amen.

LESSON 5

RESURRECTION SCHEME OF THINGS

The Approach

I'm surprised when people openly admit that they do not believe in God.

I'm taken aback when people consciously, and with some form of reasoning, reject the existence of something beyond the material world. The overwhelming majority of people who have ever lived have believed in some form of transcendence or divinity or enlightenment, some kind of truth that is "out there." Even though we live in an increasingly post-Christian culture, belief in God remains high. According to a 2024 Pew Research report, only 4 percent of Americans claim to be atheists.[1] The numbers are much higher in Western Europe, but in the United States, theism in a broad sense is a belief shared by most people.

And yet nothing was more surprising to me than when a Christian pastor in our town resigned his position, announcing that he no longer believed in the God of the Bible. For two years, he had fulfilled his vocation to the best of his ability as a pastor who did not believe in God, but in the end, he could no longer carry on the charade. In a blog post describing how he came to reject belief in God and the Christian faith, he wrote,

> Imagine two folders in your brain. One folder contains all the things that strengthen faith and the other folder contains all the things about God that we don't understand (God-mandated genocide, Torah-endorsed slavery, heaven's command to kill babies, etc.). For me, and for years, the folder that contained faith-strengthening evidence was far larger than the folder containing faith-depleting evidence. . . . One by one, without me even really being aware of it, things in the first folder were making their way into the second folder. Faith-building passages in the Bible were becoming faith-depleting passages. The folders were tearing. . . . I did not lose (or abandon) my faith because I wanted to justify an unholy lifestyle. I lost my faith in the course of doing my job as a pastor. I lost my faith by studying the Bible.[2]

I interacted with this pastor on a couple of occasions before his resignation and never knew about his intellectual struggles with Scripture and the core tenets of the Christian faith. I wish we had developed the kind of relationship where we could talk about how to interpret the Bible in a way that builds our faith and how to wrestle honestly with doubt. I'm confident that all the quotations in his "faith-depleting" folder have been answered at some time during the church's history. The foundations of our faith include intellectual evidence for the existence of God and the truth of Jesus established on the foundation of his historical resurrection. I would have loved to introduce him to this great theological tradition.

Take a moment to reflect on the following questions.

1. What do you do when you have doubts or questions about core tenets of the Christian faith?

2. Why do you think people choose atheism?

3. Have you ever wondered, *What if Jesus didn't rise from the dead? What if the entire story of Jesus' death, resurrection, and ascension was fabricated by devoted followers who wanted to honor the memory of a wise Jewish prophet?* What do you do with those questions?

The Word

In 1 Corinthians 15, Paul presents us with his most compelling case for the centrality of the resurrection. If Jesus did not historically rise from the dead, then everything we believe about Jesus is, as Paul says, all "smoke and mirrors" (1 Corinthians 15:14). Paul doesn't try to prove the resurrection of Jesus in this passage. Rather, he establishes the necessity of the phenomena of resurrection to disprove those who deny its possibility. According to New Testament scholar Gordon Fee, "To deny the resurrection of the dead is to deny the resurrection of the one who makes any and all resurrections possible."[3] Let's jump into Paul's explanation of the necessity of resurrection.

> If there's no resurrection, there's no living Christ. And face it—if there's no resurrection for Christ, everything we've told you is smoke and mirrors, and everything you've staked your life on is smoke and mirrors. Not only that, but we would be guilty of telling a string of barefaced lies about God, all these affidavits we passed on to you verifying that God raised up Christ—sheer fabrications, if there's no resurrection.
>
> 1 CORINTHIANS 15:13-15

Paul writes emphatically with these words. If resurrection at the end of the age is an impossibility, then Jesus was not raised, and the apostolic witness is nothing more than a cleverly devised hoax.

> If corpses can't be raised, then Christ wasn't, because he was indeed dead. And if Christ weren't raised, then all you're doing is wandering about in the dark, as lost as ever. It's even worse for those who died hoping in Christ and resurrection, because they're already in their graves. If all we get out of Christ is a little inspiration for a few short years, we're a pretty sorry lot.
>
> 1 CORINTHIANS 15:16-19

The Christian faith isn't rooted in wishful thinking or fleeting inspiration. It's grounded in and held together by something much more secure. The resurrection of Jesus stands as the linchpin of our faith, the moment when death gave way to new creation. Without Jesus' resurrection, we are "wandering about in the dark."

> But the truth is that Christ *has* been raised up, the first in a long legacy of those who are going to leave the cemeteries.
>
> 1 CORINTHIANS 15:20

Poetic language, like what we read from *The Message* in this verse, has the power to stir our imaginations with the right combination of words. Most English translations use a phrase like *the firstfruits of those who have died* here, but *The Message* gives us the image of people leaving cemeteries—not as subhuman zombies but as full human beings reflecting the glory of the risen Jesus.

> There is a nice symmetry in this: Death initially came by a man, and resurrection from death came by a man. Everybody dies in Adam; everybody comes alive in Christ.
>
> 1 CORINTHIANS 15:21-22

There's a beautiful rhythm in these words—loss and restoration, death and resurrection. Adam's story reminds us of our frailty. Jesus' resurrection tells a new story, one where life triumphs over death and grace gets the final word. Adam's introduction of death has been rewritten by the life of the risen one.

> But we have to wait our turn: Christ is first, then those with him at his Coming, the grand consummation when, after crushing the opposition, he hands over his kingdom to God the Father.
>
> 1 CORINTHIANS 15:23-24

Jesus was sent by God the Father in the power of the Spirit to proclaim, announce, and inaugurate the Kingdom of God, and in the end, Jesus will fulfill that mission.

> He won't let up until the last enemy is down—and the very last enemy is death! As the psalmist said, "He laid them low, one and all; he walked all over them." When Scripture says that "he walked all over them," it's obvious that he couldn't at the same time be walked on. When everything and everyone is finally under God's rule, the Son will step down, taking his place with everyone else, showing that God's rule is absolutely comprehensive—a perfect ending!
>
> 1 CORINTHIANS 15:25-28

Fear of death no longer has a hold on us. We recognize death as an uninvited guest, an intruder into God's good creation. Death isn't our friend; it's our enemy. God is in the life-giving business, so life is a great and reliable friend. Let's skip down to verse 35.

> Some skeptic is sure to ask, "Show me how resurrection works. Give me a diagram; draw me a picture. What does this 'resurrection body' look like?" If you look at this question closely, you realize how absurd it is. There are no diagrams for this kind of thing. We do have a parallel experience in gardening. You plant a "dead" seed; soon there is a flourishing plant. There is no visual likeness between seed and plant. You could never guess what a tomato would look like by looking at a tomato seed. What we plant in the soil and what grows out of it don't look anything alike. The dead body that we bury in the ground and the resurrection body that comes from it will be dramatically different.
>
> You will notice that the variety of bodies is stunning. Just as there are different kinds of seeds, there are different kinds of bodies—humans, animals, birds, fish—each unprecedented in its form. You get a hint at the diversity of resurrection glory by looking at the diversity of bodies not only on earth but in the skies—sun, moon, stars—all these varieties of beauty and brightness. And we're only looking at pre-resurrection "seeds"—who can imagine what the resurrection "plants" will be like!
>
> 1 CORINTHIANS 15:35-41

We have some freedom to speculate about what a resurrected body looks like because we are given no clear description in Scripture. How can you imagine an oak tree coming from an acorn or a juicy, ripe tomato from a tomato seed? We are constrained by our imaginations, and ultimately all our speculations will be incomplete.

> This image of planting a dead seed and raising a live plant is a mere sketch at best, but perhaps it will help in approaching the mystery of the resurrection body—but only if you keep in mind that when we're raised, we're raised for *good*, alive forever! The corpse that's planted is no beauty, but when it's raised, it's glorious. Put in the ground weak, it comes up powerful. The seed sown is natural; the seed grown is supernatural—same seed, same body, but what a difference from when it goes down in physical mortality to when it is raised up in spiritual immortality!
>
> 1 CORINTHIANS 15:42-44

While we speculate and wrestle with holy mysteries, what we do know is that the body that God will raise is going to be a glorious, supernatural body marked by immortality. A supernatural body, or "spiritual immortality," does not mean a ghost-like figure but a body animated by the Holy Spirit. In the age to come, we will not need to be filled with the Holy Spirit as we are now because our very flesh will be infused with the Spirit. Let's skip down to verse 51.

> But let me tell you something wonderful, a mystery I'll probably never fully understand. We're not all going to die—*but* we are all going to be changed. You hear a blast to end all blasts from a trumpet, and in the time that you look up and blink your eyes—it's over. On signal from that trumpet from heaven, the dead will be up and out of their graves, beyond the reach of death, never to die again. At the same moment and in the same way, we'll all be changed.
>
> 1 CORINTHIANS 15:51-52

When Jesus appears, we will all be changed—not removed *from* the earth but remade *with* the earth. What God does with our physical bodies at the end is a sign of what God will do with the heavens and the earth. God will remake and renew it all!

> In the resurrection scheme of things, this has to happen: everything perishable taken off the shelves and replaced by the imperishable, this mortal replaced by the immortal. Then the saying will come true:
>
> > Death swallowed by triumphant Life!
> > Who got the last word, oh, Death?
> > Oh, Death, who's afraid of you now?
>
> It was sin that made death so frightening and law-code guilt that gave sin its leverage, its destructive power. But now in a single victorious stroke of Life, all three—sin, guilt, death—are gone, the gift of our Master, Jesus Christ. Thank God!
>
> 1 CORINTHIANS 15:53-57

God's "resurrection scheme of things" is to do away with death and make all things new. God raised Jesus from the dead as a demonstration of God's desire for new creation. Resurrection is more than coming back to life. Resurrection means undergoing a transformation from mortality to immortality, from an old creation that was subject to death to a new creation teeming with life.

Take a moment to reflect on the following questions.

4. Why is the resurrection of Jesus the linchpin of our faith?

5. How does the image of "a long legacy of those who are going to leave the cemeteries" strike you?

6. If death is an intruder and an uninvited guest, then how do we come to terms with the inevitability of death?

7. How do the images of a seed and a plant help us develop a Christian imagination for our bodies now in contrast to our resurrected bodies?

8. How does God's work of new creation sum up the "resurrection scheme of things"?

The Neighborhood

I live right off a historic street in our town with beautifully restored old homes and large, mature trees lining the sidewalk. These trees provide shade in the summer and brilliant colors during the autumn months. Beautiful flower beds lie at both ends of this historic street, cared for by the St. Joseph Garden Club, a volunteer group of neighbors who tend to these small slices of beauty in our neighborhood. In the winter, the flowers in these flower beds die, but in the springtime, they come alive.

What in your neighborhood has died and needs to be brought back to life? Perhaps it is a neighborhood flower bed that has been dormant for a couple of years. Maybe it is a holiday neighborhood tradition that has long been forgotten. Or maybe simple pleasantries that were once commonplace have diminished. The practice of resurrection is bringing back to life that which has been dead.

9. List things in your neighborhood that used to be vibrant but have disappeared or things you wish existed in your neighborhood.

10. What steps can you take to begin to implement those things you listed above?

The Prayer

As you think about practicing resurrection in your neighborhood, offer this prayer.

Creator-God, we acknowledge that you are the Author of life and not death. Transform our neighborhoods into sources of beauty and justice to bless our neighbors. Give us the creativity and spirit to initiate new life where we live. May people see our good works of resurrection life and praise not us but the God who made us. In Jesus' name we pray, amen.

LESSON 6

EMBRACE CHRIST AND BE EMBRACED BY HIM

The Approach

I don't want merely to know *about* God; I want to know God.

In C. S. Lewis's short fantasy novel *The Great Divorce*, departed souls in hell live in a dreary, desolate place known as "the grey town." A bus takes some of these souls to a beautiful, lush, green land, which they soon learn is heaven. When they arrive at their destination—the vibrant, grassy country—they discover that they are ghosts. Bright, luminous people, who they call the "Solid People" or "bright people," come to meet them. The book's narrator overhears one of the ghosts and one of the bright people engaging in a theological discussion.

At one point the bright person says, "I have come a long journey to meet you. You have seen Hell: you are in sight of Heaven. Will you, even now, repent and believe?" The ghost responds that he does indeed believe and that his religion is something he holds dear.

The bright person then invites the ghost to join him on a trek up into the mountains, where he can meet God. The bright person says, "I will bring you to the land not of questions but of answers, and you shall see the face of God." He continues his appeal, "Hitherto you have experienced truth only with the abstract intellect. I will bring you where you can taste it like honey and be embraced by it as by a bridegroom."[1]

The ghost is hesitant and resists the invitation with arguments and intellectual misdirection. In the end, the ghost refuses to go on the mountain adventure to see God because he remembers he has a paper to deliver at a theological society back in the grey town. *How ironic!* This sad soul doesn't want to meet God face-to-face because he must go present an academic paper about God. He finds more comfort in his ideas about God than in standing in the very presence of God.

Don't get me wrong; I love theology. I love learning about who God is and what God is doing in the world. But more than obtaining information, I want to know God—up close and personal. Accumulation of God facts in and of itself does not equate to experiencing the living God because God is not an object in the universe to be studied. We cannot see God with our best telescopes or microscopes. We encounter God and know God as a gift of grace exercised by faith; this process entails the work of our hearts as much as our heads.

I'm not saying we should set aside all intellectual pursuits. Far from it! "Wise men and women are always learning, / always listening for fresh insights" (Proverbs 18:15), and what we do in Bible studies like this one unveils this God made known in Jesus through Scripture. But knowing the Bible is not the same thing as knowing God.

Jesus describes experiential knowledge of God using the phrase *eternal life*. In his high priestly prayer in John 17, Jesus says,

> This is the real and eternal life:
> That they know you,
> The one and only true God,
> And Jesus Christ, whom you sent.
>
> JOHN 17:3

To have the kind of spiritual receptors that enable us to know God, we must first know ourselves—our whole selves, not just our bodies. Our bodies certainly bear the goodness of God because everything God makes is good. Nevertheless, we are both body *and* soul. We are indeed hybrid creatures, each possessing a physical *and* a spiritual nature. We each have a complex interior life that we keep hidden from the world, and it requires self-awareness and self-reflection to access that part of our humanity.

Self-awareness is one of many steps toward God awareness. And the good news, according to the Orthodox bishop and teacher Kallistos Ware, is that "God is far better than the best that we know in ourselves."[2] Knowing one's self is not an attempt to discover God locked away in the inner rooms of our hearts but rather to develop the sensibility to come into contact with true realities outside the sensory world. The skills needed to know ourselves help us in our pursuit of knowing God.

Take a moment to reflect on the following questions.

1. What are the differences between knowing *about* God and knowing God?

2. What are some of the skills of self-awareness that would help you draw near to God experientially?

3. Think back to some of the moments of your life when you've experienced a deep encounter with the living God. What did you take away from those encounters?

The Word

The apostle Paul wrote Philippians from a prison, presumably in Ephesus. Paul admits that "all the soldiers here, and everyone else, too, found out that I'm in jail because of this Messiah" (Philippians 1:13). Despite the chains of its author's imprisonment, this apostolic letter is marked by joy. Paul found joy in his incarceration and more joy in his love for the church in Philippi. In *The New Testament in Its World*, authors N. T. Wright and Michael Bird write, "Paul displays heartfelt gratitude to the Philippians, whom he regards as nothing less than his joy and crown. Indeed, this letter goes to show that Paul remained tied with bonds of affection to his churches."[3] Paul took joy in his imprisonment, in the church, and in his knowledge of God.

This joy was not the result of cheap amusement. This joy had come through hardship. Paul had found himself harassed by several groups as he was planting new churches in the ancient Mediterranean world. Paul had worked to plant intentionally multiethnic churches, places where Jewish and non-Jewish people worshiped Jesus together.

Some first-century Jewish followers of Jesus wanted Gentiles to observe Jewish customs, like male circumcision. Paul did not consider these people real believers because true believers in Jesus were led by the Spirit to leave behind Jewish markers of participation in the life of the new people of God.

Paul's exhortation to the Philippians regarding those pushing Jewish customs was strong! Let's take a look.

> Steer clear of the barking dogs, those religious busybodies, all bark and no bite. All they're interested in is appearances—knife-happy circumcisers, I call them. The *real* believers are the ones the Spirit of God leads to work away at this ministry, filling the air with Christ's praise as we do it.
>
> PHILIPPIANS 3:2-3

The new people of God formed by Jesus through the establishment of a new covenant were made up of Jews *and* Gentiles, worshiping together, marked not by the outer circumcision of the flesh but the inward circumcision of the heart. According to Paul in Romans 2, becoming a member of God's covenant community was a matter of allegiance to Jesus as the Messiah and the mark of God on the heart. The "knife-happy circumcisers" were Jewish Christians who were forcing Jewish traditions on non-Jewish Christians.

> We couldn't carry this off by our own efforts, and we know it—even though we can list what many might think are impressive credentials. You know my pedigree: a legitimate birth, circumcised on the eighth day; an Israelite from the elite tribe of Benjamin; a strict and devout adherent to God's law; a fiery defender of the purity of my religion, even to the point of persecuting the church; a meticulous observer of everything set down in God's law Book.
>
> PHILIPPIANS 3:3-6

With these words, Paul established his authority as a committed Christian leader rooted in a legitimate Jewish tradition. He had been a Pharisee, a member of a conservative purity movement driven by a desire to live strictly according to Jewish law.

The Pharisees weren't all bad. They were motivated by a love for the Torah, "God's law Book," filled with God's instructions for God's people; Jesus and his family would have identified with the Pharisees' devotion to the Torah. Sadly, many within the Pharisee clan had become hypocrites, playactors, pretenders, and manipulators who had forgotten the heart of the law, which is summed up in love. Jesus saw the moral rot within this conservative movement. Pharisees played the role of self-appointed defenders of the purity of their religion—as Paul, before his encounter with Jesus, had—but they neglected justice, kindness, faithfulness, mercy, and empathy (Matthew 23:23-24). They knew the laws of God but did not know the Spirit of God.

> The very credentials these people are waving around as something special, I'm tearing up and throwing out with the trash—along with everything else I used to take credit for. And why? Because of Christ.
>
> PHILIPPIANS 3:7

Paul, courageously, was willing to throw out all his Jewish credentials, to renounce his family ties to a religion in which he'd been born and bred, to throw away all he had achieved as a Pharisee. Why? One word: *Jesus*. Paul had had a real encounter with the living God through Jesus Christ. This revelation of Jesus had quite literally knocked him off his feet. Once Paul had seen God up close, he could never go back and see himself from the point of view formed by his Jewish identity.

> Yes, all the things I once thought were so important are gone from my life. Compared to the high privilege of knowing Christ Jesus as my Master, firsthand, everything I once thought I had going for me is insignificant—dog dung. I've dumped it all in the trash so that I could embrace Christ and be embraced by him. I didn't want some petty, inferior brand of righteousness that comes from keeping a list of rules when I could get the robust kind that comes from trusting Christ—*God's* righteousness.
>
> PHILIPPIANS 3:8-9

The Message's use of the phrase *dog dung* not only has striking alliteration to it but also provides more of a rhetorical punch than the word *rubbish*, seen in many modern translations (e.g., ESV, NASB, NKJV, NRSV). The Greek word used here is the common term for anything that was considered waste, like animal feces. Paul's experiential knowledge of Jesus was so overwhelming that nothing—*absolutely nothing*—compared to it. Paul had experienced the risen Jesus. He could no longer embrace the traditions of his past. He cast them aside so he could "embrace Christ and be embraced by him"—a mutual and affectionate experience.

> I gave up all that inferior stuff so I could know Christ personally, experience his resurrection power, be a partner in his suffering, and go all the way with him to death itself. If there was any way to get in on the resurrection from the dead, I wanted to do it.
>
> PHILIPPIANS 3:10-11

Experiencing resurrection power in knowing Jesus does not make us exempt from suffering—it certainly didn't for Paul. We find no new life *without death*, no gain *without suffering loss*, and no resurrection *without crucifixion*. Along with Paul, we, too, have experienced Jesus' resurrection power and get to partner with Jesus in his suffering. Resurrection power is the ability to see God and a world that is not directly in front of us, a world whose Builder and Maker is God.

Take a moment to reflect on the following questions.

4. What are the differences between external and internal markers of covenant membership for the people of God?

5. What are the problems with hypocritical, defensive, purity-obsessed, legalistic religion?

6. What have you had to set aside or give up to be an authentic follower of Jesus?

7. Why do we try to bypass suffering on the way to prosperity? Why is it that we are drawn to resurrection but want nothing to do with crucifixion?

8. How does the light of the resurrection of Jesus help us see and know God in a personal way?

The Neighborhood

Nearly all people want to connect to something bigger than themselves; that includes our neighbors. The fancy term for this in philosophical and theological circles is *transcendence*. Deep within the human heart lives an impulse to reach out to *something* out there, whether it be the "universe" or a cause to belong to or a movement to join. I'm convinced that this desire is the desire for God. "I don't believe in God, but I miss Him" is the opening line to Julian Barnes's 2008 memoir *Nothing to Be Frightened Of*.[4] Barnes, an award-winning British author, vulnerably conveys this longing for transcendence. I believe people all around us—in quiet corners of the neighborhood and on busy streets—live with this longing. Our responsibility is to bear witness to Jesus, the only one who can satisfy this desire.

9. Who in your neighborhood has expressed a similar longing to what I describe here?

10. How can you bear witness to Jesus in a relational way with those in your neighborhood?

The Prayer

As you think of those who are still looking for the satisfaction and significance we find in knowing Jesus, offer this prayer.

God of all creation, you have made all things, and all you have made is good. May we know you in the power of the resurrection and partner with you in your sufferings. Inspire us by the Holy Spirit with creative ways to be your presence in the lives of people around us so that they may seek you and find you. In Jesus' name we pray, amen.

LESSON 7

LIVING THIS NEW RESURRECTION LIFE

The Approach

I am a task-oriented person, and as a pastor, I understand that people are my task.

Early in my career, when I was blinded by my own drive to accomplish goals and feel successful, I—unfortunately—overlooked many of the people in my congregation, particularly the quiet ones, the hurting and vulnerable ones. I fell into the trap of building a successful organization instead of cultivating a community out of strangers. And then Eugene Peterson came into my life, helping me reimage my calling. In *Five Smooth Stones for Pastoral Work*, Peterson exhorts, "Pastoral work is interested in people and their failure to achieve the humanity that is theirs by the will of the God who created them. The pastor who works with such people sees them not as a unicellular organism but as 'members of the body.'"[1] Peterson's words came at the right time. Pastoral work isn't about getting things done but loving people well. These people—God's people—are not cogs in a machine or individual consumers;

they are beloved members of a body. "We need community," according to Peterson, "to complete our humanity."[2]

Shepherding and serving the people of God, a community of faith, is the task given to pastors and church leaders. Such a statement should go without saying, but it's easy to lose sight of this mission in an individualistic, consumer-driven culture that rewards accomplishment and success. I began to recalibrate my self-reflection as a pastor because of a new imagination the Holy Spirit created in me. No doubt the Spirit used the writings of Eugene Peterson, but I know that the Spirit has been at work making me new for decades. Paul writes, "So we're not giving up. How could we! Even though on the outside it often looks like things are falling apart on us, on the inside, where God is making new life, not a day goes by without his unfolding grace" (2 Corinthians 4:16).

Becoming a new person living a new life has been made possible by the resurrection of Jesus. Think of the resurrection of Jesus as an event in history that created a wormhole in the space-time continuum. (Working with this metaphor will require a science fiction imagination.) A wormhole is a theoretical tunnel or passageway through space and time that allows travelers to move quickly through both. Wormholes have been featured in movies like *Interstellar* (2014), *The Avengers* (2012), and *Contact* (1997; based on the novel by Carl Sagan). Hypothetically, a wormhole would allow you to travel quickly from one point in time and space to another, more distant point, much like the phenomenon of hyperspace in the *Star Wars* films.

Imagine the resurrection as Jesus going into death and creating a wormhole from this broken-down world into God's new world, where all things are restored. In this sense, the resurrection of Jesus opens up a doorway into a new life. We step into the opening of this wormhole at our baptism, and we continue to pass through it throughout our lives as we pursue Jesus.

As we step into God's new world, we become new creatures. We become people of love who love God with all we have and love one another with deep affection. We prioritize other people and look out for the marginalized and most vulnerable among us. Making choices such as these is what it looks like to live this new resurrection life.

Take a moment to reflect on the following questions.

1. Do you like science fiction? If so, what are your favorite sci-fi movies, shows, or books? If not, what are your favorite kinds of movies or books?

2. Are you more task oriented or people oriented? Are you more satisfied when you accomplish a task or when you meet someone new?

3. When you are meeting someone new, what are some of the telltale signs that the person you are talking to is a Christian?

The Word

Paul, in Colossians, continues his habit of writing letters from prison. At the end of the letter Paul asks for prayer that he may have more opportunities to preach the gospel, the beautiful mysteries of God revealed in Jesus, which, Paul notes, "is why I am here in chains" (Colossians 4:3, NLT). He wants to share specific guidance for the Colossian believers to live in community as people of forgiveness and truth telling. He offers guidance for wives, husbands, children, servants, and masters. His apostolic admonitions are not simply universal principles or mere commonsense advice. They are realities breathed into being by the life, death, and resurrection of Jesus.

According to the apostle Paul, "God rescued us from dead-end alleys and dark dungeons. He's set us up in the kingdom of the Son he loves so much" (Colossians 1:13). He continues, "We look at this Son and see the God who cannot be seen. We look at this Son and see God's original purpose in everything created" (Colossians 1:15). Jesus "moved into the neighborhood" (John 1:14) and lived among us for thirty years as a common workaday carpenter. His hands bore the calluses of hard work. And in his flesh, tanned by the sun, the presence of the living God could be found. As God, Jesus created all things and holds all things together: "So spacious is he, so expansive, that everything of God finds its proper place in him without crowding" (Colossians 1:19).

The revelation of God incarnate in Jesus shone so bright in the mind of Paul that anything he wrote about how we should live as the people of Jesus was shaped by the person of Jesus. We live because Jesus is alive. We rise to new resurrection life because God raised the Son from the dead. It's upon this foundation that Paul offers his counsel to the Colossians.

> My counsel for you is simple and straightforward: Just go ahead with what you've been given. You received Christ Jesus, the Master; now *live* him. You're deeply rooted in him. You're well constructed upon him. You know your way around the faith. Now do what you've been taught. School's out; quit studying the subject and start *living* it! And let your living spill over into thanksgiving.
>
> COLOSSIANS 2:6-7

As we grow in our understanding of the Kingdom of God, the Bible, and theology, our goal in the pursuit of knowing God is not mastery of the subject but mirroring of the life of Jesus. Receiving Jesus as Master and Lord is only the first step. Upon receiving him, we grow roots deep into Jesus and the two-thousand-year tradition built around Jesus and kept alive by the church. A flowering bush doesn't grow roots just to have roots. The roots allow the plant to stand firm so it can bloom. We bloom from the brilliance of the life *of* Jesus when our roots are established *in* Jesus.

> Watch out for people who try to dazzle you with big words and intellectual double-talk. They want to drag you off into endless arguments that never amount to anything. They spread their ideas through the empty traditions of human beings and the empty superstitions of spirit beings. But that's not the way of Christ.
>
> COLOSSIANS 2:8

"Big words and intellectual double-talk" serves as a helpful translation of this verse. The Greek word *philosophia*, used here, is the source of the English word *philosophy*. Paul's writings regularly include phrases and ways of thinking that reveal Paul's working knowledge of Greek philosophy. Paul wasn't trying to tell first-century Christians to avoid philosophy altogether. Rather, Paul warned followers of Jesus against the dangers of endless arguments, superstitions, and ideas rooted in empty traditions. The problem wasn't—and isn't—philosophy itself but bad philosophy communicated in unfamiliar intellectual words spoken to draw people away from Jesus.

> Everything of God gets expressed in him, so you can see and hear him clearly. You don't need a telescope, a microscope, or a horoscope to realize the fullness of Christ, and the emptiness of the universe without him. When you come to him, that fullness comes together for you, too. His power extends over everything.
>
> COLOSSIANS 2:9-10

Everything we need to know about God can be seen in Jesus. As we have seen, "We look at this Son and see the God who cannot be seen" (Colossians 1:15). From the beginning, when so-called doubting Thomas saw the risen Jesus, touched his wounds, and declared, "My Lord and my God!" (John 20:28, NLT), the followers of Jesus collectively believed in the full divinity of Jesus. While powerful telescopes allow us to see the beauty of the universe, they—along with microscopes and horoscopes—do little to help us realize how empty the universe would be without the presence of King Jesus!

> Entering into this fullness is not something you figure out or achieve. It's not a matter of being circumcised or keeping a long list of laws. No, you're already *in*—insiders—not through some secretive initiation rite but rather through what Christ has already gone through for you, destroying the power of sin. If it's an initiation ritual you're after, you've already been through it by submitting to baptism. Going under the water was a burial of your old life; coming up out of it was a resurrection, God raising you from the dead as he did Christ.
>
> COLOSSIANS 2:11-12

The ancient people of God under the old covenant saw male circumcision as the marker of membership in God's covenant community. In Jesus, this sign has been refashioned into two related markers—baptism and faith in Jesus. God has raised us from the dead through baptism, just as God raised Jesus to new life. Baptism has become a *new* exodus for the *new* people of God, made up of both Jews and Gentiles. We passed through the Red Sea, where not the Egyptians but our old lives were drowned. We were subsequently raised into a reimagined Promised Land, one of peace, love, and joy—a new, fruitful life in Jesus.

> When you were stuck in your old sin-dead life, you were incapable of responding to God. God brought you alive—right along with Christ! Think of it! All sins forgiven, the slate wiped clean, that old arrest warrant canceled and nailed to

> Christ's cross. He stripped all the spiritual tyrants in the universe of their sham authority at the Cross and marched them naked through the streets.
>
> COLOSSIANS 2:13-15

The NLT translates Colossians 2:13 as "You were dead because of your sins," and *The Message* helps us understand what that kind of death means. We were dead in the sense that we were incapable, in and of ourselves, to respond to God. We were like sheep without a shepherd, people in need of help! God moved into the neighborhood and forgave our sins, defeating all the tyrants—sin, death, and the devil.

> So if you're serious about living this new resurrection life with Christ, *act* like it. Pursue the things over which Christ presides. Don't shuffle along, eyes to the ground, absorbed with the things right in front of you. Look up, and be alert to what is going on around Christ—that's where the action is. See things from *his* perspective.
>
> COLOSSIANS 3:1-2

Are you serious about living this new resurrection life? Completing an eight-lesson Bible study on the subject is a positive indication of your seriousness. But simply learning about resurrection life is different from *living* resurrection life. If you *are* serious, then live it! Jesus is alive. Look up! See what's happening in the Kingdom of God, where Jesus rules and reigns. Begin to look at the world with new eyes—resurrection eyes—just like Jesus does.

Take a moment to reflect on the following questions.

4. What does receiving Jesus look like? What does rooting yourself in Jesus look like?

5. Why might some people be drawn away from the truth in Jesus by "big words" and "intellectual double-talk"?

6. When we see Jesus at work in the Gospel books, what do we see about the character and nature of the unseen God?

7. In what ways was your baptism an exodus into a new way of life?

8. What does it mean for you to see with "resurrection eyes"—to see things from Jesus' perspective?

The Neighborhood

When Jesus moved into the neighborhood, he did so to proclaim the Kingdom of God, which brought a new set of priorities, a realigned set of values. Jesus said, "Do you want to stand out? Then step down. Be a servant. If you puff yourself up, you'll get the wind knocked out of you. But if you're content to simply be yourself, your life will count for plenty" (Matthew 23:11-12). To be great in God's new world illuminated by resurrection light, we need to step back from our efforts of self-promotion and become servants. When our attention is on ourselves, we fail to see our neighbors. When you look around in your neighborhood, are you looking for ways to avoid your neighbors or to serve them?

9. How does the resurrection of Jesus empower us to be servant minded?

10. What are some of the practical things you can do to serve your neighbors?

The Prayer

With tangible ways to serve your neighbors in mind, offer this brief prayer.

O God, our Redeemer, you are the God who brings new life into dead spaces. Thank you for sending Jesus to redeem and restore what has been broken in our lives and in our neighborhoods. As we seek to root our lives in the life of Jesus, give us resurrection eyes so that we may see the needs around us, and give us hearts ready to serve. In Jesus' name we pray, amen.

LESSON 8

MAKING EVERYTHING NEW

The Approach

I confess my faith every day using the words of the Apostles' Creed.

Confession in a Christian context is the act of confessing our sins, a helpful practice for growing in grace. James exhorts us, "Make this your common practice: Confess your sins to each other and pray for each other so that you can live together whole and healed" (James 5:16). I confess my sins in prayer every day and have made it a practice to confess my sins and failures to other people, particularly when I have sinned against them. But the practice of confession has two sides, and confessing our sin is only one side of the coin.

Not only do we confess our sins, but we also confess our faith. The Greek word translated "confession" in the New Testament is *homologia*, which is made up of two words: *homo* (meaning "same") and *logia* (meaning "word" or "saying"). When we confess our sins, we are saying about our sin what God says about it—namely, that sin is destructive. When we confess our faith, we are saying the same thing about the Christian faith that Christians have been saying since the beginning. The writer of Hebrews encourages us to persist in our confession of faith, saying, "Since then we have a great high priest who has passed through the heavens, Jesus, the Son of God, let us hold fast our confession [*homologia*]" (Hebrews 4:14, ESV). The ancient creeds of the church—particularly the Apostles' Creed, the Nicene Creed, and the Athanasian Creed—have stood the test of time as reliable confessions of our shared Christian faith.

My journey toward faith in Jesus began among sincere people who loved the Bible but had little interest in the historic creeds of the Christian faith. At that time, I associated the practice of reciting creeds with meaningless tradition, boring worship services, and pointless ritual. When I was young, I neither understood the value of tradition nor recognized the traditions present in my own local church. I wrongly assumed that tradition itself was to be avoided, not realizing that we all have traditions, rituals, and habits that shape us. What I naïvely viewed as the lifeless recitation of a creed has turned into a life-giving practice. In the words of the late Rich Mullins regarding the Apostles' Creed, "I did not make it; no, it is making me."[1]

Now that I'm more than thirty years invested in the Chrisitan faith, what I have come to appreciate about the creeds is that the regular practice of using them to confess our faith helps us get the end of the Christian story right. The Bible tells a story from original creation to *new* creation. If the Bible were a screenplay, I imagine it would have five acts:

Act 1: Creation
Act 2: Corruption
Act 3: Covenant
Act 4: Christ
Act 5: New Creation

While the Bible contains different kinds of writing, from history to poetry, its overarching narrative tells a single story, from God creating the world and all that is in it to the re-creation of heaven and earth. The end of God's story—and therefore the end of *our* stories—is not fire, destruction, and an undoing of the world. Rather, if we are reconciled to God through faith in Jesus, this end means the resurrection of our bodies and life everlasting, our new selves planted and flourishing in God's renewed earth.

When we put our faith in Christ Jesus, we find our names written into the story of new creation. If we are in Christ, we are re-created because we join the work of God, which is to make all things new. Jesus calls us to realign ourselves with his mission because the Kingdom of God comes to establish a new covenant, a new people, and a new vision of the future. We can now cast aside the fear that our broken and sin-sick world will always stay the same. The hope that we confess is that in Jesus "the old life is gone; a new life emerges!" (2 Corinthians 5:17).

Take a moment to reflect on the following questions.

1. Did you grow up in a church that recited creeds? If so, as you look back, do you find value in it? If not, what were some of the traditions your church practiced on a regular basis?

2. As you look to the future of the church, what emotions arise in you? Are you filled with hope, concern, pessimism, some mixture of all three, or something else entirely?

3. Why is the practice of confessing both your sins and your faith necessary to grow in Christlikeness?

The Word

God began the final phase of the new-creation project with the resurrection of Jesus. God raised Jesus from the dead as a signpost. In his resurrection, Jesus "stands first in the line of humanity he restored. We see the original and intended shape of our lives there in him" (Romans 8:29). Jesus' death and subsequent resurrection were only the start. God is going to raise to life a new humanity, people of faith who trust in Jesus. By faith we are raised with Jesus, and by the power of the Holy Spirit we are transformed into the image of Jesus. We become new creatures in Christ, no longer misshaped by a hostile and self-absorbed culture.

And our re-creation signals the dawn of what's to come. The God who raised Jesus from the dead—and us with him—intends to raise all creation into new life.

This announcement is how our story begins: "First this: God created the Heavens and Earth—all you see, all you don't see" (Genesis 1:1). At the end of creation, God rested, and "God looked over everything he had made; / it was so good, so very good!" (Genesis 1:31). The stamp of goodness upon the Creator's creation has never been completely erased, even if the creatures made in God's image have worked tirelessly to wipe it out.

Whenever I catch a sunrise on an early-morning run through the parkway in our city or I find myself far away from the lights of the city on a summer night and glimpse the starry sky, I'm reminded that God's creation is good. God plans on restoring the goodness of creation. This vision of new creation is the end of our story. It was prophesied by Isaiah (Isaiah 65:17), was proclaimed by Peter (2 Peter 3:13), and is beautifully described in the second-to-last chapter in the last book of our Bibles.

Let's explore how the Bible tells the end of our story.

> I saw Heaven and earth new-created. Gone the first Heaven, gone the first earth, gone the sea.
>
> REVELATION 21:1

As a master craftsman, God has no plans of wadding up the world and tossing it into a cosmic trash can. Never! God's plan is to do away with the old order of things in the world, so in that sense, heaven and earth as we know it will be gone. But the newly fashioned heaven and earth will be healed and repaired, which is why our work to make our communities better has such value. Anytime we advocate for justice, serve those who struggle with food or housing insecurity, or care for those who are sick, broken, lonely, abused, or imprisoned, we are doing the work of new creation.

> I saw Holy Jerusalem, new-created, descending resplendent out of Heaven, as ready for God as a bride for her husband.
>
> REVELATION 21:2

With the building of the Temple in the Old Testament, the ancient city of Jerusalem served as a sacred emblem of God's dwelling place with God's people. The psalmist declares, "I'll complete what I promised God I'd do, / and I'll do it in company with his people, / In the place of worship, in God's house, / in Jerusalem, God's city. / Hallelujah!" (Psalm 116:18-19). In the final installment of new creation, the old Jerusalem will be replaced with a new Jerusalem, one descending from heaven to earth.

> I heard a voice thunder from the Throne: "Look! Look! God has moved into the neighborhood, making his home with men and women! They're his people, he's their God. He'll wipe every tear from their eyes. Death is gone for good—tears gone, crying gone, pain gone—all the first order of things gone." The Enthroned continued, "Look! I'm making everything new. Write it all down—each word dependable and accurate."
>
> REVELATION 21:3-5

In a final act of grace, God will do again what God did in the beginning of the gospel story—God will move into the neighborhood. In the end, God joins us in new life—*resurrection life!*—just as God in Jesus joined us in life through the incarnation and death through the crucifixion. God will be with us always, and there in God's new Jerusalem, when our feet are planted firmly on God's new earth, God will forever remove the source of human sorrow and suffering, problems and pain. Death will be done away with. God will finish the work of making everything new. Let's skip down to Revelation 21:21 for one final glimpse of God's promised restoration.

> The main street of the City was pure gold, translucent as glass. But there was no sign of a Temple, for the Lord God—the Sovereign-Strong—and the Lamb are the Temple. The City doesn't need sun or moon for light. God's Glory is its light, the Lamb its lamp! The nations will walk in its light and earth's kings bring in their splendor. Its gates will never be shut by day, and there won't be any night. They'll bring the glory and honor of the nations into the City. Nothing dirty or defiled will get into the City, and no one who defiles or deceives. Only those whose names are written in the Lamb's Book of Life will get in.
>
> REVELATION 21:21-27

One part of the newness in the age to come will be the replacement of the Temple and even the sun itself. Jesus, "God's Passover Lamb!" (John 1:30), will be our temple. The glory of God shining brightly from the face of Jesus will be the only light we need. There's no need for exclusion in the age to come because the peace of God will be offered to all. Everyone who truly wants to enter will be welcomed in. Nothing will defile that city. Those whose robes have been "scrubbed . . . clean in the blood of the Lamb" (Revelation 7:14) will find a seat at the table because their reservation will have been secured in the Book of Life. All the nations in this newly created earth will live by the light of Jesus, and the gates to the city will never be shut.

Take a moment to reflect on the following questions.

4. Why is it important to get the end of the Christian story right?

5. What are the differences between God removing us from the world to destroy it and God coming to earth to make everything new? What are the implications of these two contrasting visions of the future?

6. How does our care for the sick, broken, lonely, abused, or imprisoned demonstrate God's work of new creation?

7. What hope do you derive from this new-creation vision of no more tears, pain, or death?

8. What aspects of this vision of new creation cause you to rethink what you have believed about God and how God works in the world?

The Neighborhood

My neighborhood sits adjacent to Mount Auburn Cemetery, where people have been buried for nearly two hundred years. From the second-story window in my home office, I can see a rolling hill and tombstones in neat lines. Living next to a cemetery reminds me that death hasn't been completely abolished. That cemetery remains active throughout the year.

I doubt any of us can claim that our neighborhoods look anything like the picture of the newly created City of Light we read about in Revelation 21. We still see pain in our neighborhoods. We still shed tears in these places where we live. We wrestle on a regular basis with the hope of the future and the pain in the present, but we choose not to fall into despair. God has moved into our neighborhoods, and God is at work. The question is whether we have the courage to work with God in making everything new.

9. What are some of the key problems or areas of brokenness you see in your neighborhood?

10. What can you do in your neighborhood to work with God in making things new?

The Prayer

As you reflect on God's new-creation project, offer the following prayer.

O God, you know our weaknesses, our problems, and our pain. We rejoice that you have joined us in this resurrection life. Come now and make things new. Come in the power of your Spirit to renew our hearts and minds. Come in the kindness of your grace and make things new in our neighborhoods. Bring healing, comfort, freedom, and peace. All for your name's sake, amen.

AS WE GO

We've completed our walk through eight passages of Scripture. Once again, the beauty of *The Message* translation has helped bring to the surface some details in the Scriptures that may have been buried in the linguistic sand. Our meditation on the power of the resurrection of Jesus is a helpful practice during the season of Easter, and it continues to fill our lives with hope throughout the year. When a time of deep reflection on the resurrection of Jesus comes to an end, I feel lighter, less burdened, and more motivated to worship our God, who is not the God of the dead but the God of the living!

The collection of psalms in the Old Testament has been—and still is—a treasure trove of prayers and songs for the people of God. The Psalms give us vocabulary for praise. In light of our exploration of the resurrection of Jesus, my heart was drawn to these lines from Psalm 30:

> All you saints! Sing your hearts out to God!
>   Thank him to his face!
> He gets angry once in a while, but across
>   a lifetime there is only love.
> The nights of crying your eyes out
>   give way to days of laughter.
>
> PSALM 30:4-5

We often interpret the hardships and suffering of life as effects of the anger of God. We silently ask, *Why is God mad at me?* When it looks like everything is falling apart and the very ground beneath us seems like it's giving way, it can feel like God has abandoned us, as if God has "dump[ed us] / miles from nowhere" (Psalm 22:1). It may even feel like we are being crucified. It's true that we experience nights filled with tears, but heartache and pain are never the end of any of our stories because pain wasn't the end of Jesus' story. Jesus rose from the dead so that our "nights of crying" would "give way to days of laughter."

What we discover on the other side of our resurrection is that our entire lives have been filled with love, the love of God that never leaves us. Feel the pain when it comes, but take hope that one day pain will be no more because death itself will be no more. May this ancient hope fill you and sustain you. As you walk the streets of your neighborhood, may this resurrection light of hope pierce through the darkness of the lives of your neighbors. May this hope open a door for the gospel so that others may know the love of God revealed in Jesus and be transformed just as we are being transformed.

ACKNOWLEDGMENTS

I am a believer in the power of the Holy Spirit to work with Holy Scripture when the holy people of God study and discuss Scripture together. To that end, I have been writing Bible study discussion questions for the local church for decades. I have added reflection questions to all the books I have written. For years I have written discussion questions for groups to wrestle with together alongside the content of the sermons at my local church. I've been humbled by the kind responses from individuals and groups of people who have found my questions thought-provoking and helpful. The God in the Neighborhood Bible Studies are my first attempt at a comprehensive, multivolume Bible study written for the local church for individual and group use. I'm grateful for the support and encouragement of so many who have made these Bible studies possible.

I'm grateful for the team at NavPress. As a high school student, I participated in The 2:7 Series discipleship course published by NavPress, and now, some thirty years later, I'm thrilled to be able to write a Bible study series to add to the NavPress catalog of discipleship resources. I appreciate the enthusiasm of David Zimmerman and Olivia Eldredge for this project. Since the first day I pitched the idea for a Bible study using the beauty and particularity of *The Message*, you have both given me unwavering support. Olivia, it has been a joy to work with you in the editorial process. You have a strong sense for how readers engage with the Scriptures and with my writing and reflection questions. Your keen insights and constant encouragement have made my writing better. Yay! Thanks to Elizabeth Schroll for your careful editorial work. It has been a true pleasure to work with you on this project.

Thank you also to the number of people who gave me feedback on titling and content for these studies. I'm grateful to Joe Beach, who shares a love for Eugene Peterson and *The Message*, for his suggestions and input. Thanks to fellow author and Bible study enthusiast Kat Armstrong for reading my first lesson and providing me with helpful feedback. Thanks also to the members of Word of Life Church in St. Joseph, Missouri, who attended many of the Bible studies I led during Advent 2023 and Eastertide 2024. Your discussions during those Bible studies gave shape to this series.

An unmistakable thank you is due to my wife, Jenni, who remains my faithful confidant and supporter. Thank you for giving up many Fridays when I was tucked away writing these Bible studies. Thanks to my sons, Wesley, Taylor, and Dylan. One book in this series is dedicated to each of you with a blessing. Each of you, in your own way, makes me so proud! Thank you to Maggie and my grandsons, Leo and Sam, for rounding out the Vreeland clan. I love you all so much. Thanks to my brother, Jeff, and my father, Ed, for all your support and for cheering me along as I write.

Finally, I'm deeply grateful for the impact Eugene Peterson has had on my life as a pastor, author, lover of Scripture, and follower of Jesus. My family gave me a copy of *The Message Devotional Bible* for Father's Day some time ago. While I had regularly referenced *The Message* over the years, I hadn't taken the time to read it daily until 2023 and 2024. I looked forward to my Bible reading during that season because *The Message Devotional Bible* not only provided me with Peterson's helpful contemporary translation but also offered notes from him along the way. I treasured spending those mornings with Eugene and his beautiful translation. These Bible studies, using *The Message*, are a way for me to extend my gratitude and to help, in a small way, to keep the life and legacy of Eugene Peterson alive. I love you, Eugene. Thanks for showing me the way.

NOTES

AS WE BEGIN | AN INTRODUCTION TO RESURRECTION

1. See Eugene Peterson, "A Sort of Homecoming," *The Message Devotional Bible: Featuring Notes and Reflections from Eugene H. Peterson* (NavPress, 2018), 1069.
2. "Language and the way we use it in the Christian community are the focus of this conversation on the spirituality of language. Language, all of it—every vowel, every consonant—is a gift of God. . . . I want to tear down the fences that we have erected between language that deals with God and language that deals with the people around us. It is, after all, the same language." Eugene Peterson, *Tell It Slant: A Conversation on the Language of Jesus in His Stories and Prayers* (Eerdmans, 2008), 2, 4.

LESSON 1 | THE ONE WHO GIVES ME BACK MY LIFE

1. N. T. Wright, *The Resurrection of the Son of God*, Christian Origins and the Question of God, vol. 3 (Fortress Press, 2003), 31.

LESSON 2 | I AM, RIGHT NOW, RESURRECTION AND LIFE

1. Karen Stiller, *Holiness Here: Searching for God in the Ordinary Events of Everyday Life* (NavPress, 2024), 147.

LESSON 3 | OUR NEW GRACE-SOVEREIGN COUNTRY

1. Kübler-Ross developed this paradigm from her study of patients coming to terms with terminal diagnoses, but it can be a helpful framework for understanding how we process the deaths of loved ones. Kübler-Ross "publicly acknowledged . . . that the stages were not meant to be linear" and "asserted that several stages might occur simultaneously, be skipped, or not occur at all." For more on the stages of grief, see Dr. Allan Kellehear, "Dr. Elisabeth Kübler-Ross and the Five Stages of Grief," Elisabeth Kübler-Ross Foundation, accessed September 17, 2025, https://www.ekrfoundation.org/5-stages-of-grief/5-stages-grief.
2. David Kessler, *Finding Meaning: The Sixth Stage of Grief* (Scribner, 2020), 7.
3. Walter Brueggemann, "Status Quo," short film, The Work of the People, accessed August 5, 2025, https://www.theworkofthepeople.com/status-quo.

LESSON 4 | YOUR EVERYDAY, ORDINARY LIFE

1. N. T. Wright and Michael Bird describe these chapter divisions. See N. T. Wright and Michael F. Bird, *The New Testament in Its World: An Introduction to the History, Literature, and Theology of the First Christians* (Zondervan Academic, 2019), 509–10.

LESSON 5 | RESURRECTION SCHEME OF THINGS

1. Michael Lipka et al., "8 Facts About Atheists," Pew Research Center, February 7, 2024, https://www.pewresearch.org/short-reads/2024/02/07/8-facts-about-atheists.
2. This blog post was subsequently deleted. I wrote down the quote beforehand.
3. Gordon D. Fee, *The First Epistle to the Corinthians*, rev. ed., *The New International Commentary on the New Testament* (Eerdmans, 2014), 822.

LESSON 6 | EMBRACE CHRIST AND BE EMBRACED BY HIM

1. C. S. Lewis, *The Great Divorce* in *The Complete C. S. Lewis Signature Classics* (HarperCollins, 2007), 486–87.
2. Kallistos Ware, *The Orthodox Way*, rev. ed. (St. Vladimir's Seminary Press, 1995), 28.
3. N. T. Wright and Michael F. Bird, *The New Testament in Its World: An Introduction to the History, Literature, and Theology of the First Christians* (Zondervan Academic, 2019), 434.
4. Julian Barnes, *Nothing to Be Frightened Of* (Vintage International, 2009), 3.

LESSON 7 | LIVING THIS NEW RESURRECTION LIFE

1. Eugene H. Peterson, *Five Smooth Stones for Pastoral Work* (Eerdmans, 1992), 194.
2. Peterson, *Five Smooth Stones*, 192.

LESSON 8 | MAKING EVERYTHING NEW

1. "Creed," by Rich Mullins (with David "Beaker" Strasser), track 5 on *A Liturgy, a Legacy & a Ragamuffin Band*, Reunion Records, 1993.

God in the Neighborhood Bible Studies

The God in the Neighborhood Bible Studies revisit the incarnation, crucifixion, and resurrection of Jesus in fresh ways with real-life applications. Each study uses the beautiful text of *The Message* and has eight lessons that can be used individually or with a group.

1. *Incarnation* dives deep into the mystery of the incarnation, where God joins us in life.
2. *Crucifixion* reflects on Jesus' execution, where God joins us in death.
3. *Resurrection* leads us through the Easter story, where God joins us in life anew.

Author Derek Vreeland helps us draw close to Jesus so that our lives may be transformed by him.

Available at NavPress.com and wherever books are sold.

NavPress
Bold. Loving. Sensible.™
Published in alliance with Tyndale House Publishers

CP2083